The Modern Guide to Sexual Etiquette for Proper Gentlemen & Ladies

DOUBLE EAGLE
Publishers

The Modern Guide to Sexual Etiquette for Proper Gentlemen & Ladies

Written and Illustrated by

Tom Carey

First published January 1987

10

Manufactured in the United States of America

ISBN: 0-943084-53-9

Published by
DOUBLE EAGLE, INC.
1124 N. Derbyshire
Arlington Hts., IL 60004

To anyone who has ever heard those five little words, "Was it good for you?"...

...and had the good grace to lie.

Special thanks must go to these fine people who, inadvertantly or not, have provided one or more of the following: words, phrases, concepts, inspiration, spiritual guidance and assistance with the gruelling field research.

Ray (You missed the deadline again) Strobel
Mike (House Party) Mervis
Susan (Lambs) Lamoreaux
Eric (The Fish) Ramsey
Bob, his pet sheep
Jim (Peeg Dog) Regula
Mike and Judy (Couple of the 80's) Rodell
Linda Kenney and her "married lady underwear"
Jeff (The headboard device) Gardner
Terry (WD) Loch
Michael (I'm not taking you home tonight) Chiappetta
Jane (Fingers) Sicurella
Charles (The French Lover) Tackes
Jim (The Party King) Nolte and the Josemobile
Pam (It Must Be Him!) Johnson
Spiny Norman
"Gland" Meharg
Davis Scott
Steve (HSMM) Hoshor
Dennis Clair
"Bad" Bob Tencer
Freddie's Down the Road
Mike (Man is King) Caporale
The Vail Lounge

And to anyone else who thinks they recognize themselves herein. It's just a coincidence. Honest.

Why don't we get drunk and screw? I just bought a waterbed,
it's filled up with Elmer's Glue.

—Jimmy Buffet

TABLE OF CONTENTS

WHY DID SOMEONE BUY THIS BOOK FOR <u>YOU</u>?

Chances are very good, due to the nature of the material contained herein, someone bought this book for you as a gift. Chances are very good they're trying to tell you something. Chances are what they're trying to tell you is that you make love with all the grace of a skewered wildebeest.

Well maybe not. Maybe it's just a little joke. Maybe they're just having a bit of fun at your expense. Perhaps you'll all have a good laugh and then you'll toss this little volume aside.

But think carefully.

Are you really so sure of yourself? Are you confident with all the dating and mating rituals of our society or do you handle yourself with all the grace and elegance of Larry, Moe and/or Curly?

Are you smooth, suave and confident in bed or do you commit sexual errors and breaches of etiquette so gross and outrageous that your partner becomes physically ill at the mere thought of grappling with your naked body?

Can you really afford not to read further?

Don't you ever wonder why it is you haven't had a date, an intimate relationship or even a cheap, tawdry one nighter since Milton Berle was funny?

I think it might be better for all of us if you'd wake up and smell the coffee!

Now stop blubbering and turn the page.

WHY THIS BOOK?
An Introduction

The social/sexual whirl can be an awesome and frightening experience for beginner and scarred veteran alike. Often, during these turbulent and confusing times, it is unclear what one's social responsibilities really are. It is especially difficult nowadays, when so many people, young and old, married and single, spend so much time and energy pursuing each other for purposes of selfish physical gratification.

It's become increasingly clear to me that an etiquette guide for the sexually promiscuous...oops, I mean sexually active, is necessary—indispensible really—for anyone slugging it out in the war between the sexes.

Questions answered herein; from "What side of the bed do I take on a One Night Stand?" and "Do I really have to swallow?" have just *not* been covered thoroughly by Miss Manners and Emily Post.*

With all the problems confronting the lone Don Quixote, tilting at the windmills of the sexual conventions of this world, my best advice is to stay at home with a bowl of popcorn and a really good book. If you must venture into the land of herpes and heartbreak then let *this* really good book be your guide. You still may end up with herpes and heartbreak, or worse, but at least you will remain comfortable in the knowledge that you'll be enduring these indignities politely.

This is by no means a how-to book. Lord knows there are enough of those around. Bookstore shelves literally sag under the weight of each new season's releases. These helpful tomes sport snappy titles like "How to Pick Up Women Even if You're Fat, Homely and Smell Like a Tannery" and "Autoerotica and You: 101 Positions for a Rainy Weekend."

Instead I have concerned myself, in this snappily titled and helpful tome, not so much with *how* to have sex, per se, but how to have sex politely. I suspect most of you reading this have been having sex, alone or with others, for years and pretty much already know *how*. But, perhaps you have wondered, while sucking on the toes of someone you met 40 minutes before in a sleazy bar, "Is this really *polite*?"

As you will soon discover, there *are* socially correct ways to meet members of the opposite sex, encourage advances of members of the opposite sex, and coax bodily fluids from members of the opposite sex on to the bedclothes.

Since I have noticed an alarming rise in the vast numbers of people who are just not comfortable with the etiquette of sex, I've been moved to pen this little guide; for the benefit of my fellow man (and woman) and for a modest advance from my publisher.

Now, if you'll all just pay attention, you'll never have to worry about a new partner exclaiming "You want me to do *what* with my Cuisinart?!"

*By the way, the answer to the above questions are "The side closest to the door" and "Hell, yes."

POLITE TERMINOLOGY
What the Hell do you call THAT?

He's the missing link, the kitchen sink,
Eleven on a scale of ten,
Honey let me introduce you to my
Red Neck Friend.

                                        —Jackson Browne

POLITE TERMINOLOGY
What the Hell Do You Call That?

There are correct and incorrect ways to refer to parts of the human anatomy. Humans, over the years, have developed nicknames for their body parts, especially the more sexual ones, to avoid having to use embarrassing words like "penis" and "vagina," and "perineum." Actually we don't really need any name at all for the perineum because people rarely speak of this area of the body. Unless they have developed an uncomfortable rash.

Men, in particular, love to have little pet names for sexual parts. Women rarely refer to their sex organ as "my sweet honey pot of golden desire." Men, however, do. If you don't believe me, read a copy of Penthouse Letters.

Men also have little pet names for women's breasts, legs and buttocks. And, of course, they name their own parts. *Especially* their own parts. The following list is only partial. No doubt you can think of dozens more on your own.

The Heat Seeking Moisture Missile

The One-Eyed Anaconda

The Bishop and His Nice Red Hat

The Tube Snake

The Hose Monster

Junior

The Big Guy

The Anteater (Uncircumcised only)

The Trouser Trout

My Third Leg

The Blue Veiner (Erect only)

The Woody (Erect only)

The Purple Helmeted Warhead

While there is nothing particularly rude about these names, they are all rather silly and not polite for use in mixed company. If, for example, you're at dinner with an important customer, don't say to his wife, "Excuse me. I have to go to the men's room to drain the Hose Monster." Sales will plummet. You ladies should be particularly careful about associating with men who bandy these kinds of names about with frequency. Especially "Heat Seeking Moisture Missile."

Men are also tremendously fond of little pet names for the parts of women, especially those with whom they have developed a close relationship. You ladies are undoubtedly aware of the most common of these and I won't go to the trouble of listing them here. Oh, hell, sure I will. Most of them are pretty funny.

Vocabulary list

Boobs

Tits

Jugs

Bazooms

Bazongas

Hooters

Ta-tas

Winnebagos

Golden Bozos

Titters

Watermelons

Yabbos

Muchachas

Mammaries

Mambos

Love Muffins

Ear Muffs

Gazongas

Head Lights

Fried Eggs

Knockers

Casabas

Knobs

Titteroos

Oompahs

Tetons

Mounds

Rosebud tipped scoops
of vanilla ecstasy*

*not in general use

Apparently this strange compunction for nicknames derives from the proprietary interest they usually develop during a relationship. Soon after you begin dating he will name each of your breasts. Chances are they will be very silly names, maybe Fred, Herb, or Algernon. Soon after that he will name your sex organ. Do not be alarmed. Though this *is* strange behavior, it is certainly not unheard of. He may call it Bob. You will find him calling you at the office and saying "Hey, honey, I'm coming over to see the boys tonight." Humor him. Most men did not develop a suitable fantasy life when they were growing up. They're just playing house with you. If he names your sex organ "Ulysses S. Grant," "Sasquatch," or "George Carlin," you should stop seeing him and call the authorities at once.

Most men won't get this carried away, however. They'll mostly be content with talking baby talk to your breasts and maybe referring occasionally to your posterior cheeks as "my golden globes of quivering desire." Try not to laugh when he says these kinds of things. It's not polite and besides, if you do, your golden globes will quiver wildly.

BIRTH CONTROL
Polite Prevention for Prudent People

We all worry about the population explosion, but we don't worry about it at the right time.

—Arthur Hoppe

BIRTH CONTROL
Polite Prevention, Correct Contraception

The subject of birth control has always been a very sticky one. (Pun acknowledged.) Despite what ultra-conservative, paranoid elementary school board members everywhere believe, open discussion of birth control methods is very polite indeed. As a matter of fact, if there's anything more impolite than thousands of 14-year old mothers, I'm sure I don't know what it is. But that's a whole other book. The most impolite thing you *can* do, in regard to contraception, is *not* mention it. Or, even worse, not mention it until it's too late, as in "Oh, by the way Honey, I'm not using anything, but since we love each other I know everything will be all right." Or, even worse than that, not mention it until the proceedings are proceeding, as in "I'm not protected dear, so please be careful." If you care about the man you're making love with, don't give him a coronary. This sort of behavior is not proper, correct or polite in any way.

If you women of the 80's are going to have sex with every Tom Cruise look-a-like that comes along, do yourself a favor: get on the Pill, or get a diaphragm. (Or carry a gross of rubbers in your purse. It's easy to do and if you go home alone you can always fill them with water and toss them off the roof at passing vehicles.)

I realize that I'm being a bit tough on the ladies here, but let's face it girls, most men are dried, congealed ice cream on the hot vinyl car seats of life. *You* are the one who'll have to deal with an unwanted pregnancy, not him. So you have to handle the contraception. I suspect if it were men who got pregnant we'd have developed safe, effective and cheap birth control long before we got the Fuzz-Buster, the Pocket Fisherman or the In-Egg-Scrambler.

Q: I am embarrassed and at a loss as to what to do when my lover puts on his "rubber." What is the proper thing to do? Do I watch? Or help him with it?

A: It is always proper for a lady to assist a gentleman with his prophylactic. After all, it's use is a benefit to both parties. However, it is not polite to look at him and say "Gee, Honey, look how much is left rolled up at the bottom!"

Q: I'm 16 years old and I just don't know the correct thing to do. My boyfriend wants to have sex, but I'm afraid. Is there any 100% sure way of not getting pregnant?

A: Certainly. Go to your local library. Ask at the information desk where they keep their set of Encyclopedia Britannica. Find volume twelve and look up the entry for "Model T Ford." Read it carefully. Close the book and hold it between your knees.

Q: My wife prefers to use a diaphragm as a method of birth control. I, unfortunately, haven't got the faintest idea how it works. Is it correct for me to offer to help her...uh...install it?

A: Why the hell don't you ask her! It constantly amazes me that people who have vomited, broken wind, and been naked in each other's company (not to mention having swallowed various amounts of each other's bodily fluids) can still find things that they're too uncomfortable to discuss.

Be that as it may, the diaphragm is a flat, circular, rubber device that fits over the woman's cervix. It is properly accompanied by a spermacide; a gel applied to the diaphragm that insures that the few hardy little sperm that sneak by are KO's before they can do any damage. Keep in mind that it tastes a bit like industrial solvent. It's all right to help your partner insert her diaphragm but it's quite a bit trickier than putting on a prophylactic. And it's never appropriate to play Frisbee with your partner's diaphragm. Although I understand it's great fun.

Q: I'm tired of dealing with all the mess involved in using a diaphragm and I'm thinking of having an IUD put in. Is this a proper form of contraception?

A: I think the idea of having a little piece of wire or plastic floating around inside me is as appealing as chewing tin foil.

Q. I've heard a lot about the rhythm method. What about that?

A: The rhythm method was popularized by pious Catholics following the decrees of bent old men who never have sex at all. It involves, in theory, timing sex so that it takes place only on the days of the month when the woman is not fertile. After subtracting the week when she is ovulating, and the week when she's having her period, and allowing for the several days that the man's sperm can survive in her reproductive system, the rhythm method allows approximately one hour and seventeen minutes for sex. In theory.

In practice, the rhythm method involves self-control, self-denial, and cold showers for weeks on end. This results finally in an explosion of sexual frenzy, followed by tremendous, breast-beating guilt. This is closely followed by prayers for forgiveness, and shortly thereafter, birth.

Q: **A man I met recently keeps pressuring me to have sex with him. He's okay I guess, but I'm sure nothing permanent would ever come of it. The point is, he says he's had a vasectomy and I'd have nothing to worry about. Is it polite for me to ask to prove it? Can I call his doctor? Or look for a scar?**

A: You SLUT! (Oops, I forgot, this is the Eighties. Now even women can have sordid, cheap sex with someone they barely know.) Your problem is how to keep from bearing the child of a man from whom you clearly should not buy a used car.

It would be extremely rude, not to mention unethical, to try to get personal information from his doctor. Besides, it probably wouldn't work. You might give his ex-wife a call, though. She might not be able to help but I'm sure you'd both enjoy a few cheap laughs at his expense.

It would also be very rude to ask to examine his scars. I'd love to see how you intended to accomplish this, however. Perhaps with a flashlight in the nearest public restroom. Anyway, I suspect any man sleazy enough to actually say "Don't worry baby, I've had a vasectomy," is probably also sleazy enough to apply "Dr. Wizzo's Realistic Plastic Scar Make-Up" to the underside of his privates.

Q: **I'm afraid to take the Pill and my boyfriend won't use a rubber. He says it's like washing your car in a thunderstorm or something like that. Most of the time, when we make love he "pulls out." I don't really think that's very polite, do you? He** *says* **he has complete control.**

A: The breaches of etiquette in your relationship, as revealed by this pathetic letter, are so numerous that before answering I need to go take several aspirin. All right, I'm back. I'll try to limit my advice to questions of etiquette only.

First, "pulling out," or "coitus interruptus," is the single most impolite form of birth control. Not only is it rude, it's messy.

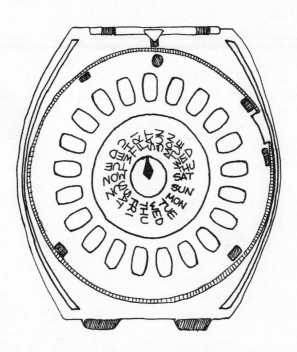

(As you've no doubt discovered.) And besides, it doesn't work. Sperm are very hard-working, crafty little buggers and some of them are liable to climb up your leg when you're not looking.

Second, get on the Pill. That way you can be completely careless and indiscriminate about letting strange men climb naked on top of you. A few women experience side-effects but the benefits far outweigh the disadvantages. (So you'll grow a mustache, chest hair and a deep love for Car and Driver magazine and chewing tobacco. A pouch of "Red Man" is a whole lot more fun than a shotgun wedding.)

Third, unload this guy. Any man who thinks that "coitus interruptus" is a satisfying sexual experience is a bonehead. Of course, from the looks of this letter, you two may deserve each other. If that's the case I have another birth control suggestion. Sterilization. For both of you.

THE HUNT
Fifty Ways to Meet Your Lover.

*Despite my thirty years research into the feminine soul, I have
not yet been able to answer...the great question that has never
been answered: What does a woman want?*

—Sigmund Freud

THE HUNT

Fifty Ways to Meet Your Lover

This section is meant primarily for those of you who are unmarried, unbetrothed or unfaithful. Or those of you who wish you were. Readers coupled in blissful ignorance may want to skip this one. Thinking of divorce? Read on and recall those halcyon days of yore when you, too, were single. Relive the joy, the adventure, the sheer terror of yet another blind date set up by your second cousin Cynthia the podiatrist's assistant and sometime rock groupie, who is shocked by the fact that you spend so many Saturday nights watching "Love Boat" reruns with only a quart Häagen Dazs Pralines and Cream for company. (That should send you screaming back to your spouse.)

Meeting someone to love, for one night, or even several, is a difficult and frightening undertaking, at best. Men, unless you're a professional athlete, high-ranking corporate executive or coke dealer, you will have to face the fact that women will not be lining up on your front porch in skimpy underclothing. And you women face the far different but no less exasperating problem of trying to tell the average nice guy apart from the average crazed serial killer on the basis of a few minutes conversation and two large margaritas. Here's a quick tip: If he says he dresses up as "Tippy the Clown" and entertains at kiddie birthday parties on the weekends, get the hell out of there and hope to God he won't remember your last name.

There are, as most single humans are no doubt aware, innumerable ways to meet a member of the opposite sex for fun, games, or to exchange bodily fluids. There's the old fashioned, reasonably safe, blind date approach, or you can go totally modern, and advertise in the classified section of the newspaper as if you were an old Dodge with bald tires and a turned back odometer. Some popular books, found primarily in grocery store check-out lines, advocate hanging around in laundromats and produce aisles to meet possible mates.

Q: How the heck would I meet a man in a laundromat or grocery store? That doesn't sound very polite.

A: What you're supposed to do is this. Wait until you see an attractive man loading his laundry. Check it for bras, nightgowns and other items of female clothing that would indicate a more than casual attachment or a penchant for cross-dressing. If everything checks out, approach the man, smile innocently and say, "I really don't know much about these machines. Could you tell me what setting I should use for these?" Then hold up a pair of red satin crotchless panties. This is a terific way to meet a man because men love to help a lady in distress. And what sane man wouldn't want a deep, spiritual relationship with a woman who displays her exotic underwear to strangers in public places?

Thanks to the modern entrepreneurial spirit, there are now combination bar/laundromats opening all over the country, for the benefit of men who like to pick up women who read these helpful little books.

Similarly, grocery stores are purported to be excellent trolling grounds for the lonely single. Try this one, men. Hang around the produce section until an attractive woman with no wedding ring stops by to squeeze the canteloupes. Affect an endearing, perplexed look and say, "Gee, I hate to bother an attractive, sensual, obviously unmarried woman like you, but do you think this 8″ cucumber of mine is about the right firmness and texture?" If she doesn't scream for the store security, you'll know there's a chance she'll want to feel your cucumber.

As you may have surmised by now, these self-help books for the desperate single person are 90% horse poop. Admit it, would you really date someone who has to ask whether a bright green tomato is ripe or not, or someone incapable of laundering their own clothes?

Q: **I've never been to a singles bar. They sure wouldn't seem to be a very safe, or proper, way to meet someone. Are singles bars considered correct as far as mate hunting goes?**

A: No. The singles bar is a scary, strange place indeed. The singles bar was invented, several years back, by an elderly philanthropist who saw the need for a place where young, unmarried folks could go to meet, talk, and feel around on each other. He also realized that such a place would be ideal for selling enormous amounts of alcohol. A reclusive and mysterious man, he made his fortune exploiting the insecurities of others, then sold out suddenly, retreating to a life of solitude in the high deserts of Arizona. This marketing and franchising genius is also responsible for bringing to America the largest restaurant franchise chain in history, *Gas Food Next Right.* I'm sure you've seen the signs along the highway.

Actually, the singles bar of the Eighties is a direct descendant of the disco bar of the seventies. Discos, in those days, were places where young people went to drink, smoke and "shake their booties." They were strange places that featured loud music, floors that lit up and machines that belched huge clouds of fog. The music, featuring bass, drums, keyboards and the sounds of Donna Summer climaxing, was played over enormously powerful sound systems by "disc jockeys." Disc jockeys were usually squat, hairy men who wore gold medallions, shirts open to the waist and skin tight polyester pants. These men used enough hair spray in the 70's to permanently damage the Earth's ozone layer. They yelled, "Yeah, baby," at least 86 times each evening.

Discos began to decline in popularity when club owners took to decorating their walls with floor to ceiling length mirrors. When people saw how ridiculous they looked when "shaking their booties," they left in droves, deeply ashamed, never to return. Mental hospitals have entire wards dedicated to the care of unfortunate souls damaged permanently in this era.

The disco itself was kind of a backlash from a previous time, a very rude era in American history, called the 60's. At this time, for some unknown reason, young people everywhere decided, all at once, to go without shaving, bathing or working. They listened to Jefferson Airplane albums at high volume. In terms of etiquette, it was a low in our country's great history. Some experts blame it on the addition of too much fluoride to the drinking water at this time.

The sexual arena of the 60's was chock-a-block with bean bag chairs, black-light posters of Jimi Hendrix, illicit smoking materials and little or no underwear. It was a scary time to be alive.

The only remnant of this tremendously rude time is the illicity smoking material which we'll cover in a later chapter. If I can just score some somewhere.

In any case, the 80's are a new era of enlightenment. One may meet a potential lover at any time and any place...cruising the YMCA, in passing buses, at the bingo parlor...but the bars remain the favorite.

Q: What's the polite way to signal to an attractive man, in a bar, that I'm interested?

A: If you're a woman, in a bar, by yourself, simply making eye contact for four-fifths of a second should do it. Many men require even less encouragement than that. In a roomful of men who have been drinking, there are bound to be some who will interpret your straightening your skirt as a sign that you want to make a video tape with them and a Siberian Husky.

Frankly, most men would be tremendously flattered if any woman were to approach them, simply introduce herself and ask to sit down. It is perfectly acceptable for you to do this. However, be aware that you will be running the same risk that men have been running for years...namely, rejection. Have you ever stared, disgusted, at a man who has just asked you to dance, with a look that says, "Not if you had a wheelbarrow full of $100 bills"? It can be very disquieting to see that look on the face of someone else. Men's hormone production being what it is, however, chances of this happening are very slim.

It is *never* polite to say, "Hey, tiger, wanna go out to the parking lot and make ten bucks the hard way?" Although I'm told this approach works, too.

Q: **Women in bars seem so defensive these days. I try to do the correct thing when meeting a lady, but it seems almost impossible. What's the polite way for me to let a gal know I'm interested in getting to know her a little better?**

A: First off, let's skip the bullshit. What you're interested in doing is getting to know the contents of her sweater a little better. Second, if you refer to her as a "gal" she may suggest you do something anatomically impossible with your imported "lite" beer bottle, (Knuckleheads who say "gal" always drink imported "lite" beer.)

The correct thing to do, gentlemen, is nada. Nothing. Zip. Until you receive at least a little encouragement. This calls for some sensitivity on your part. If she happens by your table on her way to the ladies room you may *not* consider yourself encouraged. If she strolls purposefully up to your table, fixes you with a sultry, half-lidded gaze and says, "I want to have your child," *then* you may consider yourself encouraged. Ask if you can buy her a drink. You might get lucky.

It's the subtle variations in between these approaches that seem to give men the most trouble.

I suggest that the proper gentleman always wait for at least a couple of feminine overtures, no matter how subtle. There is nothing more embarrassing than approaching a woman who you believe is giving you the eye, only to discover she's fixing a contact lens and wouldn't be seen with you even if you made large deposits to her money management account.

Those of you who are more desperate, more aggressive, or work in stereo sales may find it necessary to ignore this advice and approach women, sans invitation. Do not be surprised when you receive an icy rejection along with an icy cocktail in your lap.

Q: **I don't want to sound desperate, but is it polite for a lady to approach a gentleman she is not yet acquainted with? You know, like at a bus stop, in an elevator, or just on the street?**

A: My, my, you *do* sound desperate. Introducing yourself to strange men on the street is as safe and polite as entering an attack dog training center wearing Gainesburger underpants.

Please, please, please, ladies! Has it gotten that bad out there? I know there are polls out in every magazine these days trumpeting the supposed "man shortage," but has it come to this? There *are* eligible men out there. Trust me, I know. They're driving fork lifts and shoveling pig entrails in the factories and on the farms from coast-to-coast in this great land of ours. They're out there swearing and spitting and wearing sweat-stained baseball caps with Caterpillar Tractor emblems on them. They love football and deep-fried anything and they need you to pick up their dirty socks and to fetch them "brewskies."

Oh. You wanted to meet an intelligent, compassionate, attractive and clean man? One who'll scoop you up in his arms and whisk you away from your dreary life as a secretary in an industrial waste disposal plant to live a life of luxury in his Swiss chalet?

In that case, you'll have to live with the poll results.

Q: **Well, maybe placing an ad in the personal section is the way to go. Is it correct to advertise myself in the paper? Or to answer an ad?**

A: I must confess that modern etiquette is not quite up to speed as far as the "personal ads" go. In other words, I haven't got around to making up the rules yet. I do, however, have a few guidelines for those of you desperate enough and shameless enough to respond to those ads.

1. A woman who describes herself as "Rubenesque" weighs at least 210 pounds.

2. Any man looking for a "discreet" relationship is married.

3. A man who wants someone "sensual" likes to be whipped with studded belts and made to eat Kal-Kan.

4. "Tired of the singles scene" means "I never got lucky in the bars."

5. "Love good music" means "I have a complete collection of Bachman-Turner Overdrive albums."

6. "Love walking in the rain" means "I'm a romantic idiot who thinks life should be like a Hollywood musical with Gene Kelly."

7. "Race unimportant" means "I'd love to make it with a beautiful black woman named Tiger."

8. "Love trips to the zoo" means "I have two kids."

9. "Professional" means "I've been off unemployment for several weeks now."

10. "Sense of humor a must" means "My idea of a good time is a Three Stooges film festival."

THE ONE NIGHT STAND:
Politeness and Promiscuity

One should always be in love. That is the reason one should never marry.

—Oscar Wilde

THE ONE NIGHT STAND
Promiscuity and Politeness

Although slightly less common than it used to be, due to various
and sundry sexually transmitted diseases and movies like *"Looking
for Mr. Goodbar"* and *"I Spit on Your Grave,"* the One Night Stand
still enjoys a revered place in the annals of the sexual revolution. Let's
be honest now, we've all done it. (Well, *I* never have.) Waking up in
a strange room, in a strange bed, next to someone who may or may
not be strange (you really don't remember that much, do you?) can
be a very unsettling experience indeed. Fear not! There are rules of
etiquette to cover all sexual situations. You were hoping there would
be, weren't you?

First, ladies, you can save yourselves lots of trouble by observing
these simple guidelines when out in a man-meeting situation.

1. Avoid men who wear so many gold chains around their necks
   that they are permanently discolored.

2. Avoid men who say "Gee, I hope they don't tow here, my Cor-
   vette is double-parked."

3. Avoid men who smoke long, thin, brown cigarettes with French
   names.

4. Avoid men whose sideburns exceed 8" in length.

5. Avoid men who use mousse.

6. Avoid men who thump their bellies proudly and belch.

7. Avoid men who talk about their ex-wive's sexual shortcomings
   in detail.

8. Avoid men who wear T-shirts with clever sayings on them like "I'm With Stupid" or "Sit on my face and I'll guess your weight."

9. Avoid men who order "Double Harvey Wallbanger for me and a white wine and Dr. Pepper for the little lady."

10. Avoid men with visible nose hair.

I have also compiled a handy list of guidelines for you men.

1. Avoid women who wear more than seven earrings.

2. Avoid women who say "Shit, I had to park my Harley out in the open. It better not fuckin' rain."

3. Avoid women who smoke corn cob pipes.

4. Avoid women whose hair is one of the primary colors.

5. Avoid women who wear "beehive" hairdos.

6. Avoid women with tattoos.

7. Avoid women who wear "long-line" bras. Outside their clothing.

8. Avoid women who talk about their ex-husband's sexual short-comings in detail.

9. Avoid women who order "Shirley Temple, extra garbage."

10. Avoid women with visible armpit hair.

Q: If we *do* manage to find someone and we decide to "go for it," who decides where we should go?

A: First, I must point out that your prospects of finding someone to enjoy a healthy, meaningful sexual relationship with in a dark, smoke shrouded bar at 3 a.m. are as dim as the cocktail waitress. But then, you already knew that, didn't you?

So, it's last call, and you think you've found someone to whom you wish to do strange things with your tongue. That person seems agreeable. You gaze deeply into each other's eyes and each of you yearns to say those magic little words. "Your place, or mine?"

The polite thing to do is to let the lady decide. Their are two schools of thought among women on this one. Some want to be at their own home because it makes them feel more comfortable. If you're going to be stumbling around naked in the middle of the night looking to use the bathroom, you like it to be your own bathroom.

There are drawbacks, however, to being at home. You may wake up in the morning looking at the naked body of someone you wish didn't have your address. Plus, you may want him to leave after he fulfills your carnal desires whereas he may decide to fall asleep across three-quarters of the bed and your left leg.

On the other hand, there are those women who prefer to accompany the man to his home. There, you can cut your losses and leave anytime. The drawback here is that many bachelors believe that changing bed sheets more than once a season is a waste of time and that greasy pizza cartons piled on the stove top are sort of "homey."

Yes the world of the One Night Stand is fraught with peril. The truly polite never get drunk and pick up strangers in a bar to take home with them. The truly polite go to a fine hotel.

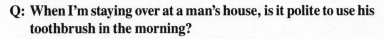

Q: When I'm staying over at a man's house, is it polite to use his toothbrush in the morning?

A: Think of all the disgusting things he was doing with his mouth last night. You *know* he's done those things many times before with many different people. Do you really still want to use his toothbrush?

Q: What side of the bed should I take on a One Night Stand?

A: The one nearest the door.

POLITE DATING
Looking for Mr. Goodmanners

"Drive-in, ya guzzle gin, commit a little mortal sin…yeah it's good for your soul."

—*Jimmy Buffett*

DATING
Looking for Mr. Goodmanners

Now, suppose you get through all this silliness and actually find someone you're interested in leaping on top of naked. And, it turns out, they're actually interested in the same thing. How does one proceed from here? How does one progress from "Hello" to "Oh, God, move your leg to the left and stick your finger in my ear!"?

There is only one time tested method in this country. It is called "dating." The mere mention of the word strikes horror into the hearts of single people everywhere.

The strange custom of dating is native only to the United States. More sophisticated cultures than our own arrange marriages at birth to eliminate this barbaric ritual. Our society would be wise to adopt this practice. It would end most of the traumas of young adulthood. Far fewer women would spend their evenings hovering over the phone, snarfing Sara Lee Cherry Cheesecake and listening to Vicki Carr sing "It Must Be Him." Far fewer prematurely balding men would comb 18 inch strands of hair across the tops of their skulls trying desperately to look young again. Members of both sexes could spend their time in healthy productive functions instead of spending it hunched over half empty scotch glasses and muttering to themselves in dimly lit bars.

Unfortunately for us, the advertising industry has a tremendous stake in keeping single people everywhere scared to death about their weight, clothing, smell and appearance. Insecure people are easy people to sell toupees, health club memberships and Lean Cuisine "Chipped Beef in a Bag" to. For this reason we in the U.S. will be stuck forever with dating. Of course, you could always enter the convent.

Good manners are especially important on dates because they allow you to conduct yourself in a dignified, proper way even after you've discovered that your date is every bit as appealing as an intestinal fluke. And has the same effect on you physically.

Does she fart audibly when the waiter recommends the coq a vin? Does he amuse himself throughout the evening by trying to toss ice cubes down the front of your dress? A truly polite person deals with these kinds of situations with tact and aplomb. Once the date is over you can go home to a nice bath, relax, call the local lawn maintenance service and order a half ton of manure dumped on your date's front lawn.

Q: Are there certain procedures I should follow to ensure that I am behaving correctly on a date?

A: First, we must define what we mean by the term "date." (Actually, I think everyone is pretty much aware of what a date is, but I'm going to explain it anyway because it's so much fun.) A "date" is what two people do together while they try to decide if they should have sex or not. Generally, the man provides the dating portion of the evening and the woman provides the deciding portion of the evening.

Normally, dating takes place in trendy, fern filled restaurants where, even if your date turns out to be a complete bozo, you can at least get a nice prime rib. Mostly these restaurants are fun, happy places with names like "Scamps 'n' Scalawags" and "Froggy Freddie's Bar, Grill, Eating Emporium and Fish Hatchery." They always have old highway signs, stuffed hoot owls and other ridiculous knick-knacks hanging from the ceiling and nailed to the wall. These things come from a restaurant supply catalog called "Stupid Stuff to Hang in Your Restaurant." It features license plates from the early Fifties, barber poles and wax statues of Grover Cleveland. All these items are strategically placed in the restaurant by a restaurant psychologist who arranges them to make it uncomfortable for you to do anything but order, eat quickly and get the hell out of there so they can turn the table.

The waiters and waitresses have to pass a verbal "perkiness" test before they are hired. They say things like, "Hi, I'm Jason, your sniveling, obsequious, bisexual waiter and I'd *love* to take your drink order." They're all just *super* happy to be working at Froggie Freddie's and prove it by singing and dancing and bringing out a birthday cake with a sparkler on top of it every ten minutes or so, whether it's somebody's birthday or not.

There is almost no way to deal with these people in a polite way. They are going to be sickeningly cheery all night and will wheel enormous carts laden with huge slabs of various baked goods to your table every sixteen seconds and plead with you to try some carrot cake.

My advice is to drink heavily and endure. With any luck, the sex portion of the evening should come just after the carrot cake portion.

Q: **What is the correct thing to do after dinner?**

A: It depends. If dinner was at one of these trendy little places, go to the bar and slosh down a pitcher of margaritas. This will get you both in the mood. After that it's pretty much up to you. A ride in the moonlight is always nice. If you drive a 1976 Honda Civic you'll need to have two pitchers of margaritas first. If you drive a Jaguar XKE you can skip the drinks altogether and go straight home to have sex. If you flew in in a Cessna for a quick dinner at Pierre's on the Wharf you should have had the sex already on the way in. Now you're free to enjoy the rest of the evening. Go bowling or play some miniature golf.

Q: **So dating mostly has to do with what kind of transportation is used?**

A: No, the transportation only affects whether or not you'll be having sex later. Anyone can date.

Q: **You mean a woman decides whether or not she'll have sex with me because of the car I drive? That doesn't seem right. Or polite.**

A: Of course it does. If women were to fornicate higgledy-piggledy with the kind of men who drive old Ambassadors or VW Vans they

would be responsible for passing those men's chromosomes on to the next generation. Who needs that kind of contamination in the gene pool? Our species must progress if it's going to survive and thrive.

Q: **My friends are always trying to set me up, but I am skeptical. Are there special rules about being polite to a blind date?**

A: Blind dates can be very tricky encounters and are definitely not for the faint of heart. The most important thing to do is to check out the friend who wants to set you up on the blind date. If she is married to an animal shelter custodian named Zbiegniev or Ray Bob you should think twice about the date.

Should you succumb to loneliness (and to the fact that you can't bear to face another night of "Dallas" and dirty laundry) keep in mind that blind dates are the perfect breeding ground for all kinds of social faux pas. Dating is rude enough without foisting yourself on someone you've never met before.

Q: **What if my blind date shows up and I know by just looking at him that it will never work? Is there a polite way to get out of it?**

A: Hell no! I warned you! If a man who weighs 400 pounds shows up at your door at the appointed time with candy and flowers, you cannot speak to him in a Czechoslovakian accent and pretend you're the cleaning lady. You are honor bound to go out with him. Even if he's already scarfed the candy.

You may not scream, "Aaaugh! I thought Orson Wells was dead!" and slam the door in his face. Just because you could launch C-47 cargo planes off a man doesn't mean that, deep down inside, he's not a wonderful person.

You need not, however, accompany this man anywhere you might be recognized or any place called "All-U-Can-Eat."

Do the following: Go on the date. Be sweet and charming. Then go find your friend's automobile and fill it with cement.

Q: If, after a date, I go up to his apartment with him, do I have to...uh...go all the way?

A: "Go all the way?" "Go all the way?" What in the hell kind of wimpy expression is that? What you're asking is, if you go back to a man's apartment after he's entertained you all evening at great expense, plied you liberally with alcohol and generally been charming, generous and wonderful, do you have to "make the beast with two backs" with him? ("Beast with two backs," now *there's* a euphemism!)

   The answer is...of course you do!

   Now, before the women's rights people begin screaming and wetting themselves, let me make it clear that the key phrase is *"if I go up to his apartment* do I have to?"

   Well, hell yes. When a man says, "Would you like to come up for a drink?" what he is saying, in a very subtle, polite way, is, "Do you want to make the beast with two backs?" (Boy, I love saying that.) If you answer, "Yes, I'd love to," he has every reason to expect you to "put out." (That's the euphemism Grandpa always used.)

   If you had a wonderful time but are not yet ready to waltz off to the land of Bouncy-Bouncy with him, simply have him take you home. Kiss him on the doorstep (or the lips) and say, "Gee, ___(his name here)___, I had a wonderful time eating the expensive food you bought me and drinking the expensive drinks you bought me and enjoying the expensive entertainment you provided and now I'm going to go in and call my mother to tell her all about it. Let's do it again real soon."

   Not for a moment am I suggesting, in my caustic, sarcastic way, that a lady should be expected to trade her physical favors for a night out with a gentleman. *Never* would I suggest that a lady compromise herself in this manner for the sake of a few drinks and dinner.

   Now, if he throws in flowers and a nice gift...

Q: Then it's okay to have sex on the first date?

A: Until recent years, even posing such a question would be considered the height of rudeness. In the fast moving world of the 80's, however, if you don't have sex on the first date you'll probably never have a second. This is harsh reality and you'll just have to live with it.

In the past, when a woman allowed a man a few chaste kisses, but no more, he would think to himself, "Hmmm, she must be a virgin. Think I'll ask her to marry me."

If she allowed more, he would think to himself, "Hmmm, this sure is fun. Too bad I can't ask her to marry me because she's a cheap, sleazy, disgusting slut."

So, given the choice between a prim, possibly frigid, woman and one with a normal healthy sex drive, men would almost always choose the former. Men at this time were very stupid.

Following normal procedure, the man would do the following: Buy the woman an expensive diamond ring. Spend great, huge piles of cash entertaining her, buying gifts for her family and hiring her good-for-nothing relatives to work in his sheet metal business. This was called the "engagement period" and it would last approximately one year.

During this period, the woman would become more and more coy and aloof. The man would see her less and less. By the week of the wedding she would be living in a different state under an assumed name.

By the day of the wedding, the man would be in such an advanced state of sexual frenzy that nothing could be considered safe from his advances. Not small barnyard animals. Not reasonably attractive breaded veal cutlets.

At this point, the woman, whom he hadn't seen for several months, would reappear. She would have lost weight. She would have had her hair done. She would have been made up to look like Merle Oberon. She would look more stunning than she ever had before, or ever would again. Especially to a man who has had an erection for a solid week. (Ever since "Bertha the Double-Jointed

Belly Dancer and Swedish Massage Expert" danced at his bachelor party.)

When they finally walked down the aisle (a singularly difficult undertaking for a man with a week old erection) the poor man would be prepared to leap naked in front of a locomotive for some kind of physical release. The woman would, on the other hand, not want her new hair and makeup messed.

This is precisely the effect that these ancient rituals were designed to achieve. The newlyweds would go off on a honeymoon and for the next several years the man would leap upon his new wife almost constantly to relieve the sexual tension built up over the year of courtship.

By the time he realized that having sex with a woman who keeps her flannel nightgown on, keeps the lights off, grips the sides of the bed, and says things like, "Are you through yet?" is no fun, he would have three children and a mortgage and it would be too late to do anything about it. Men, as I said, were stupid. Thank God times have changed.

After years of this nonsense, word began filtering down to single men from their married buddies in locker rooms and at poker games and such that sex in marriage was not all it was cracked up to be. Men began to wise up.

Along about this time, the early 60's I believe, women also began to discover something about sex. Mainly, that they, too, could enjoy it. Life magazine devoted an entire issue to the search for the female orgasm shortly before it folded. This social awakening was called the "sexual revolution." What that meant was that men and women were no longer willing to settle for a lifetime, or even several minutes, with a partner who was incapable of providing satisfactory orgasms. People read books, watched filmstrips and joined discussion groups to learn more about having satisfactory orgasms. Soon men and women everywhere were having orgasms together almost constantly, whether they liked each other or not. This was a tremendous sociological advance for our nation. It brought us venereal disease, wife swapping, and a divorce rate that doubled in a matter of months. It also changed dating forever.

Dating quickly evolved, from holding hands at the roller rink into what it is today—a way to test members of the opposite sex to see if they can provide satisfactory orgasms. Or at least orgasms that are almost as good as the ones you provide for yourself.

Not sleeping with someone after a date nowadays is like saying, "I have gotten to know you a little bit, and I doubt if you are capable of providing me with a decent orgasm." It is very rude. Unless, of course, he drives an unacceptable car. Then it is polite to refuse to have sex.

Q: **What is the correct way to proceed when we've dated for awhile and we wish to make it more permanent?**

A: Once you've found someone to provide you with plenty of nice orgasms you may decide that you're "in love" and you're ready to make "a commitment." You'll know you are ready to make a "commitment" when you wake up one morning and realize you haven't even thought about masturbating for a week. Also when the song "Wild Thing" by The Troggs comes on the radio and it makes you a little teary-eyed. Either of these is a sound basis for a "commitment." If you're still not sure, pick up the latest issue of Cosmopolitan. It will inevitably feature an article called "Love and Commitment" or "Why Your Man Won't Make a Commitment" or "How to Blackmail Your Man and Force Him into a Commitment by Taking Compromising Photos and Threatening to Send Them to His Boss." Each article will feature a little test that the two of you can take. Don't cheat. These tests are designed by highly competent professionals and you are bound, by law, to live by the results.

The test will have a dozen or so questions like this one.

On a vacation, you would most like to go:
  A. On a 20 mile hike through a leper colony, deep in the Peruvian jungle.
  B. To 10 day seminar on the proper use of dental floss.
  C. On a luxurious cruise through the Virgin Islands.

If you and your lover answer these questions the same, you'll know you were meant to be together to forever and always provide each other with swell orgasms.

Q: What is the correct way to ask for her hand in marriage?

A: It has become vouge recently for a man to propose to his true love in public. Renting a billboard, hiring a skywriter or having your proposal flashed on the scoreboard at the Super Bowl are all considered fashionable ways to ask someone to marry you. It seems that someone else's wedding is a perfect time to get drunk, grab a microphone and make the surprise announcement that "Me 'n' Donna Sue is gonna git hitched!" Even if Donna Sue coughs up her overcooked chicken Kiev, she'll probably recover enough to accept congratulations from everyone. She'll scream at you later, while you're puking on your rented shoes in the parking lot, but after she's had a chance to think about it, she may realize that marrying you would be far less trouble than trying to explain to 250 friends and relatives that you're a crude, obnoxious creep who drinks too much and rarely provides satisfactory orgasms.

Of course, it may be that you're such a slime ball that even a public proposal is not enough to convince her to marry you. It can be very embarrassing to have "Marry me, Jenny, my sweet" flashed on the scoreboard in the first quarter of the game, only to have "When pigs fly, Ralph" flashed on in the third.

THE FIRST TIME
A Special Section for Novices

Many people will tell you that the First Time they had sex was a romantic, touching moment of innocent youth. They will get positively dewy eyed remembering the passion and romance of a warm summer evening that was made for memories. They'll sigh and wonder if love will ever be that sweet and that pure again. They will be blowing smoke up your skirt. First Times are almost always sweaty, embarrassing and uncomfortable for everyone involved. They are painful and humiliating. Fortunately, they rarely last longer than about thirty seconds.

Good manners are essential at this difficult time. My fervent hope is that high schools everywhere will see the necessity to assign this book in all of their sex education classes. (Boy, would that pump up sales!) My other fervent hope is that those of you who are tempted to grope each other in the backseats of your parent's station wagons will overcome your desires and *stop it at once!* Sex is for mature people who have learned how to manipulate each other with it, not for love-struck, testosterone-crazed teenagers. Go home and practice by yourselves until you're 21 or until your first college mixer, whichever comes last.

Q: **My boyfriend keeps pressuring me to have sex with him. He says men get sick or something if they don't have sex enough. I love him but I really don't want to give in. How do I handle this as a proper young lady?**

A: Your instincts are correct. Don't do it! What your boyfriend is talking about is that timeworn condition commonly referred to as "blue balls." Supposedly, this happens to men who get "all dressed up with nowhere to go" too often, if you get my meaning. Teenaged boys have been telling teenaged girls this kind of crap since the Stone Age. Although there is some medical basis for this, I sincerely doubt whether your boyfriend is afflicted. He doesn't need you for physical reasons. He's already spending two hours a day locked in his room holding up the latest Playboy centerfold with one hand.

What he really wants from you is a story to tell the guys in the locker room. Actually, my guess is he's already telling the story and he only needs you to help him get some of the details straight.

Q: I'm still a virgin, but I really love my boyfriend and I know we'll get married just as soon as we both graduate next year. Wouldn't it be okay to make love now?

A: Haven't you been listening? There is nothing romantic about having a sixteen year-old french fry cook pull apart the elastic on your underwear, heave himself on top of you, and flail about wildly for 26 seconds on an old blanket late at night in an empty field. It will be painful, smelly and sweaty. You will get mosquito bites. The cops might come. You won't.

Little about being a teenager is very polite, I'm afraid, and sex is especially difficult. Teenagers are, by and large, awkward, hyper-sensitive, only partially complete human beings. All they do, normally, is eat, sleep, talk on the phone, and have sex with other teenagers when they should be holding down part-time jobs like cutting lawns or selling seeds door-to-door.

Statistics tell us that humans are losing their virginity at earlier and earlier ages. This is extremely unfortunate and very, very rude. Next time your 15 year-old daughter brings a boy home for dinner, dads, try to picture the two of them groping each other naked. Well? What are you going to do about it?

Frankly, the thought of 15 year-old people having sex grosses me out. I can't even stand to see the little buggers holding hands at the mall.

POLITE FOREPLAY
Priming the Pump

Whoever called it necking was a poor judge of anatomy.

—*Groucho Marx*

POLITE FOREPLAY
1. Necking
2. More Than Necking
3. Lots More Than Necking

Correct form requires that polite sex must *always* be preceeded by polite foreplay. Sorry about that, men. For most of you, I know, the perfect act of sex involves bowling a 650 series, wolfing down eighteen beers and two large bags of Fritos before coming home. There to be greeted by your woman who tears off her flimsy negligee and cries out "Take me right here on the kitchen floor my big man!" To be completely perfect, this fiery act of passion would be followed by about 16 hours of uninterrupted sleep. It should come as no surprise to most of you that women are demanding a bit more than that these days.

I will begin at the beginning, boys and girls, and go slowly, step-by-step, which, by the way, is the way you should go also. This section is of particular importance to you men because most women know all there is to know about foreplay already. At least those women who watch Oprah Winfrey, Phil Donahue and others of that ilk know all about it. If you watch these shows enough you'll begin to believe that the world is divided into two groups. People who get their earlobes nibbled enough and those who don't.

This section is broken down by bases, just like we used to do in junior high school. That is, first base, second base, third base, and (Holy Cow!) home run. I know several women who get tremendously turned on to this day just *watching* a baseball game. Especially if Ryne Sandburg is playing. If you're not sure about these designations, just pick up a recording of "Paradise By The Dashboard Lights" by Meatloaf. Or ask any 11-year-old.

FIRST BASE
Necking

"Necking," "making out," or "sucking face" are all rather stupid ways of referring to what mother used to call "petting." Come to think of it, "petting" is a pretty stupid name too. In mother's day of course necking was an end in itself as opposed to a means to an end.

One longs for these, more innocent, times. Even the professional terminology makes it clear that *fore*play is a mere appetzier on the menu of human sexual relations, only whetting the appetite for the maincourse. The main course itself was only invented in the early sixties. Before that all there was was kissing. Check any old movie if you don't believe me. They didn't even use tongues.

A kiss is arguably the most delicate and sensual of all sexual activities. It has been revered in song, story and legend back to the beginning of recorded time. Fairty tales tell of beautiful princesses being able to turn frogs into Princes with just a kiss. Evil spells could be broken with a kiss. The Seven Dwarfs got to French kiss Snow White all the time becuase she was under a magic spell and couldn't do anything about it.

The kiss has been immortalized on film. Think of the great screen kisses in history. Humphrey Bogart and Ingrid Bergman in "Casablanca." Burt Lancaster and Deborah Kerr in "From Here to Eternity." Woody Allen and Diane Keaton in "Annie Hall." Tom 'The Tripod' Smith and Anita Laye in "Gaping Maw of Moistness."

Beautiful moments all.

Nowadays, I'm afraid, instead of "Kiss me one last time Rick," it's "Quick, Guido, stick your tongue in my ear!" Which goes to prove that if romance is not dead it is, at least, in an oxygen tent.

Q: I just love to give my boyfriend hickies but he says he hates them. Would it be rude for me to give them to him anyway?

A: Hickies, for those who are unaware, are those small, purplish bruises created by sucking hard on someone's skin while in the throes of sexual ecstacy. They appear most often on the neck of the American teenager. They are strange and silly and are responsible for one of the most enduring and distasteful fashion trend of recent times, the turtleneck.

When you spy someone sporting these little marks it is perfectly acceptable to shout "Hey, didja lose a wrestling match with a vacuum cleaner?!" Actually I encourage this sort of comment. Hickies are a scourge on modern man and ought not to be tolerated.

Apparently, many among our misguided youth believe that if they parade around with lumpy, bruised necks, the rest of the world will realize they are sexually active and regard them with awe.

Here is a message for all of you: People who have real sex do not give one another hickies! They're too busy doing other fun things. If you insist on giving each other these silly things; realize that the message you're sending is, "We don't have real sex, we just hang around in rusted out Pontiacs with bad upholstery at drive-in movies and suck on each others necks."

Q: **I know a "Kiss is just a kiss..." but I've never been. Kissed I mean. Can practice or something? I don't want to appear rude or clumsy when I finally get my chance.**

A: A kiss can be sensual and sweet and wonderful and it's almost always one's initial sexual experience. (No, getting Mary Lou Henderson to pull her pants down when you were both five years old doesn't count.)

To many, kissing is far more intimate than a sex act of any kind. Prove this to yourself. Go to Las Vegas and hang out in a hotel lounge. There you will find call girls of many shapes, sizes and political affiliations. For the correct amount of money you will be able to get one to dress like a nun, dance up and down on your chest in cowboy boots or whip you with long strands of spaghettinni. But try to kiss her and she will be tremendously offended. She will tell you that she's saving all her kisses for her special guy, Vito. He will be the large swarthy man in the velvet jacket waiting outside in the hall. So make sure you tip her handsomely. As I said, romance lives.

Polite kissing requires two willing partners. It is very rude to leap on someone from behind on the street and plant a wet smooch on their neck. It can also be dangerous. Especially if the smoochee is a teamster named Bruno.

First kisses *do* present a special etiquette problem. They should ideally take place on a summer day in a big field of tall grass. Included ahould be 1.) a crystalline blue sky, 2.) a blanket, 3.) a loaf of bread, 4.) a jug of wine and 5.) thou. You'll want to have wildflowers in your hair and run around the field in slow motion.

In the Spring, you may substitute an empty city street in a sudden, but gentle, rainshower. In the Fall, use a park with the leaves falling gently all around you. You'll want to rake them into piles and run giggling and goo-goo-eyed into them.

In Wintertime, kiss only on a bearskin rug, in front of a crackling fire with a gentle snow falling outside.

All kissing should take place to the accompaniment of the "Love Story" or "Summer of '42" themes as performed by The 101 Strings. In Winter, substitute Nat King Cole singing "The Christmas Song."

Subsequent kissing may be done at anytime. Try to keep background music available. If necessary, buy a Walkman with two headphone jacks.

It *is* rude to do too much aggressive kissing in public. Believe me when I tell you that few people enjoy the sight of you and your loved one dangling a six inch string of saliva between your pursed lips.

Q: Okay, In understand all that stuff. But *how*, exactly, does it work?

A. Don't get huffy. I *could* start making these questions up myself and you'd be out of a job.

Polite kissing begins like this. Put a Barry Manilow record on the stereo. Arrange yourselves comfortably on a couch or love seat. Secretly spray your mouth with Binaca. Moisten your lips. Your *own* lips. Look deeply into your partner's eyes and try to imagine that he/she retains all those qualities that you cherish in a lover. Ignore the fact that he/she has a large colorful tattoo. And that he/she sculpts modern art with human ear wax. If you let these small obstacles stop you, you'll never get to kiss anybody. Glance furtively from your lover's eyes to his/her lips. Then quickly look from his/her lips back to his/her eyes again. Then again. Eyes to lips, lips to eyes. As you do this you should both be moving closer and closer to each other. Closer and closer you come until you can tell what he/she had for lunch. Then, when you are about to pass out from the dizziness and the corned beef-breath, you touch lips. That's it fans. It's all over! I don't have to write "he/she" anymore!

Try to remember you are gently caressing a person that you care about, not gnawing on a fresh ear of corn. And always remember the rules of the road. Each of you tilt your head to the right. This reduces the chance of serious, permanent head injury and facial disfigurement.

First kisses should never include tongues. They'll be plenty of time for all that disgusting slurping and licking later.

Q: This is typical, I suppose, but is there a polite way to ask my man to spend more time kissing me?

A: Unfortunately, there is no easy solution to this, almost universal problem. Men are, I'm afraid, very goal oriented. The same dynamic drive that makes him yearn to be promoted from stockman at the 7-11 to full-fledged assistant paper goods manager, makes him want to grope your more private parts only seconds after the kissing begins. Given a choice, most men, in a secret poll, responded as you might have suspected all along. 4% said they enjoyed kissing more than anything, 11% said it was better than a sock in the ear with a dead walleye and 85% said "Let's blow off this kissy-face garbage and get right to the good stuff."

There *is* a slim possibility that *you* are at fault, though. Be honest now. When he kisses you, do you kiss him back with equal fervor?

Do you participate fully, or could kissing you be likened to kissing a warm, moist washrag?

Or maybe you're too aggressive, though it's hard to believe very many men would find that objectionable. When he plants a warm, friendly, "It's nice to see you, honey," kiss on your cheek, do you respond by jamming your tongue into his mouth back to his molars? This kind of behavior is not attractive either.

And men, keep that Chapstick around. If you don't have any, ask the nearest female. Women are born into this world with a Chapstick attached to their hips. Surgical removal is as routine as circumcision these days, but the emotional attachment remains. And every woman in America carries a Chapstick at all times. Remember, chapped lips are not acceptable. If you kiss with the sensitivity of 60X sandpaper you will be a lonely person.

Q: **My boyfriend loves to kiss me and all that, but a lot of time he has bad breath, you know? What do I say?. He's so cool otherwise.**

A: A question. If you were unaware that your breath smelled like a moist herd of bison, would you want to be told? Yes, I thought so. If there's one thing more impolite than informing a loved one that they stink, it's having that loved one unleash a semi-noxious cloud of foul air into your mouth. Yuck. And if he has that gross little white spittle at the corners of his mouth, tell him about that too. I can't stand seeing people with that stuff.

SECOND BASE
More Than Necking

Okay, you've been necking for awhile. The temperature of the room begins to increase. You've changed gradually from a reasonably comfortable upright position into a horizontal one in which the circulation to several important limbs is cut off. You begin to feel the distinct flutter of passion rising in your breast. Or, it might be the distinct flutter of his hand on your breast.

For some reason, when necking, a young man's fancy inevitably turns to a young lady's breasts, those two fatty deposits that girls develop on their upper abdomens in early adolescence and lug around for the rest of their lives.

A woman's breast has only one real function. That is, nursing their offspring. How, then, did these simple mammary glands become the focus of so much intense sexual scrutiny? How did they become the single most (doublemost?) celebrated portions of the feminine anatomy? Historians have never fully investigated this strange phenomenon but I suspect it happened around the time in the early 1700's when most aristocratic ladies began wearing corsets that pushed their decolletage up under their chins. They also used to wear enormous hoop skirts, huge powdered wigs and fake facial moles. Thank goodness these strange customs all went out with the French Revolution. Someone should clue Madonna in about the fake moles though.

Q: Kissing my boyfriend is fun and stuff, but he keeps trying to go farther. Is there a polite way to fend him off without having every date turn into a wrestling match? (P.S. We're both in sophomore year.)

A: It's refreshing to read a letter from a nice clean-cut youngster like yourself with a nice clean-cut problem. Most high school sophomores want to know if four orgasms a night is normal or not.

As you are finding out, the male of the species is fixated upon the looming spectre of the female bosom. Especially if he's never really encountered a live pair before. Aside from a few dirty magazines and an occasional oil painting on black velvet at an abandoned corner gas station, your young man may rarely ever encounter even the sight of naked breasts. He has probably been obsessed with the idea of latching on to a pair since the age of ten. Strict Freudians might suggest that this yearning goes back even farther. To the time when Mom cruelly stuffed a rubber nipple into his mouth instead of the real live one he was used to.

For the teenaged male this obsession often becomes a quest. If you ever wonder why young boys wander around dazed and hunched over, eyes at half-mast, it's from looking every passing woman, from age 9 to 89, straight in the chest. Once he finally gets his hands on a pair (hmmm . . . just like water balloons, kinda) he should get a little more normal, although, thanks to our friends in the porn industry, many men retain this strange fixation throughout life. Some are stricken so badly they revert to a life of dairy farming.

Q: **My wife seems obsessed with the size of her breasts. She thinks they're too small. They seem all right to me. How can I convince her that size doesn't matter to me?**

A: I sincerely doubt she wants larger breasts for you. *You* wouldn't have to haul them around, she would. She wants them because she wants to look better, period.

There is no woman on this Earth who doesn't believe her breasts are too small, big, flat, round, pointed, saggy, etc.

All your protestations that, "Hell, honey, more than a mouthful's a waste anyhow," will not help and may cause her to hurl a tuna noodle casserole at you. Would you feel better if she said the same thing about your penis? No, I didn't think so.

Luckily, there is no real etiquette problem involved here. It is *always* rude to comment on a lady's breasts, even favorably. You don't say, "Yo, Bernice, you got great tits!" even if Bernice hasn't been able to sleep on her stomach since she was 11.

If she really has a problem with them you can offer, politely, to buy her a new pair. Implants are about $3,000.00. Find a reputable surgeon. You don't want people to look at her new figure and be reminded of Marty Feldman's eyes.

Q: **Is it correct for me to help my lover when he's trying to remove my bra? What if he's really having trouble?**

A: It's always proper for a lady to assist a gentleman with her brassiere. That is, if he's attempting to remove it from you. Not if he's trying to put it on himself.

It is silly and sometimes dangerous to sit quietly strangling on your own bra straps while he searches in vain behind you and the clasp is in the front.

THIRD BASE
Lots More Than Necking

"Third Base" is what teenagers do in the backseats of cars after they've been dating for awhile and have gotten tired of getting to second base in the backseats of cars.

Adults should never do this. In the backseats of cars or anywhere else. You grown-ups should think of "third base" as the "gentle caress that leads to the ultimate act of love." Or as the "overture to a beautiful, sensual, sexually fulfilling experience." Or it can just be thought of as "priming the pump."

Q: My husband is a fairly thoughtful lover but when it comes to, uh, penetration, he sometimes rushes things a bit. How can I get him to spend more warm-up time with me?

A: It is never polite for a gentleman to force himself on a lady who is not properly lubricated. Plus, it hurts like hell. My guess is that your hubby is just too dopey to figure it out for himself. Luckily, you have purchased this fabulous book for him and we can straighten him out.

Here's a helpful analogy for you men. What do you suppose would happen if you drained every drop of motor oil from your car, started it up and held the accelerator to the floor? Quite a mess, eh? Now, think of yourself as the piston and your lover as the cylinder. Yes, gentlemen, lubrication is vital.

See, ladies? You just have to know how to speak a man's language. (If he comes at you with a can of STP muttering about Andy Granitelli, you're on your own. I can't take responsibility for everything.)

Q: My boyfriend seems to be under the impression that stabbing at my crotch with his fingers is enjoyable for me. Do some women like this? I know what I'd rather have him do with his

fingers. **Is it polite for me to sort of redirect him?**

A: No. Just lie there and let him think he's a super love stud while he pries at your parts like a drug-crazed gynecologist. Sooner or later I'm sure you'll get tired of being tenderized like a slab of skirt steak and you'll just put his hand where you want it. This *is* proper. It would be better for both of you if you would also include a gentle explanation. Something like, "Hey, Long John Silver! You digging for gold, or what?!"

Q: **My boyfriend recently discovered the clitoris and all its wonderful functions. This is nice but sometimes he gets a bit carried away. Can I ask him to be gentler and slower with me?**

A: Use the answer to the preceding question, only change the explanation to, "Hey, Mr. Fix-it! Are you trying to sand that thing off, or what?"

By the way, in case you were wondering, the word is pronounced **clít·or·is,** not **clit·ór·is.** The accent is on the first syllable. How this would ever come up in polite conversation is beyond me, but, if it does, you will be prepared to pronounce it correctly. Even if you're still not quite sure where it is or how it works.

Though not officially included in the junior high schooler's designation of "Third Base," I think it's time we paid some attention to the manual stimulation of the male parts, as well as the female.

This can be a distasteful chore for many women at first but, like milking a cow, once you get the hang of it, it can be lots of fun. Make it a game. Hang targets on the wall. Try for new distance records. It sure beats the Wheel of Fortune.

Q: **What is the proper way to instruct my wife in the subtleties of the "hand job"? She doesn't really get it and I'm afraid my poor unit can't take much more abuse.**

A: Okay, I've had just about enough of this. Apparently, everybody in the world is doing this and nobody is doing it right. No wonder some people just skip this portion of the sex act all together and just dive right into the main even. "Look Ma! No hands!"

Here's what I want you all to do. Sit naked on your beds facing each other. Now, when I say go, I want you all to watch each other masturbate. Ready...Go! And no fair cheating! Girls, if you usually use a vibrator the size of a table leg, plug it in. Guys, if you normally drive carpet tacks into your nipples, then do that too.

All good sex books recommend mutual masturbation. It'll help you to better understand all the disgusting things your partner really wants you to do.

POLITE ORGASM
Is It Possible?

Drop your panties, Sir Edward, I cannot wait 'til lunchtime. Ooh, my nipples explode with delight.

—John Cleese

POLITE ORGASM
Is It Possible?

Okay now you've politely and safely negotiated the difficult areas of meeting a prospective partner, getting to know said partner (at least a little), actually getting into bed (or wherever) naked with said partner and are now engaging said partner in some kind of sexual acrobatics. Ideally, everyone involved is on the same timetable and all reach a satisfactory conclusion. Or several satisfactory conclusions. Then you both lean back, smile, light a cigarette and desperately try to remember each other's names.

More frequently, life is less than perfect, like most of us, and our timetables don't match up as well as we'd hope. Specifically, women enjoy taking the local, while men end up on the express.

Q: When I make love with my husband I'm only occasionally orgasmic. How can I ask him to work on his technique in a way that won't offend him?

A: In a perfect world we would all just relax and realize that the psychic comfort and physical release that we all seek in sexual relations derives from attaining an intense intimacy with another human being, not from achieving some arbitrary goal. (Boy, what a lovely thought. I should be writing greeting cards for a living.) Of course, shattering climaxes are nice, too.

A woman's climax is supposed to be an elusive, slippery little son of a gun, and frequently is when pursued by the hapless male.

Be assured, men, that the ladies, left to their own devices, are as orgasmic as Thompson machine guns. The devices I refer to are cylindrical, 10 inches long and can be found advertised in the back of women's magazines as "personal massagers." It's only when she's left to your devices, (i.e. your hands, fingers, nose, etc.) that the man-in-the-boat falls overboard.

The key, you knuckleheads, is communication. Women! Have pity on that poor man slobbering like a St. Bernard over your prone body, and tell him just exactly *what in the hell it is you want him to do!*

Here is a list of words and phrases to study and learn. Do your homework. It will pay off.

Higher

Lower

Harder

Faster

Softer

Slower

Yes

Yes

No

A little to the left.

More

More

Hurry

That's it!

Oh

Oh

Thanks...you're the best.

If you girls are under the impression that your role in the sex act is to lay back, close your eyes and let out an occasional ladylike squeak...well, I hereby sentence you to a lifetime of crude, awkward and helpless but well-meaning lovers who have hammer toes and are nicknamed Pee Wee.

For men, the road to orgasm is frequently shorter, straighter and well in excess of the speed limit. The trick is to make the trip last a bit longer. This can be quite a chore for someone who spent his entire adolescence hunched over a smiling, glossy Barbi Benton, hoping desperately that Mom wasn't going to knock on the door. Now, faced with you, a real live, naked, in-the-flesh female, one who is smiling and begging "Make me a woman, you big stud," he may experience one of two problems. A, premature ejaculation or, two, performance anxiety. Other books deal with curing these problems. I deal only with handling them with aplomb.

Q: **My husband occassionally has a problem "going off" too soon. He makes up for it in other ways and I don't really mind too much, but it bothers him alot. What is the correct thing to say in this situation?**

A: It's not polite to say "Nice shot, Mr. Macho. You clean the bedspread this time!" This will lead to problem two above.

The polite thing to do is not make a big deal about it. If he looks kind of sheepish and says "Oops," don't worry. Get yourself a beer, finish the People magazine article you were reading (the one about Burt & Loni. Will they *ever* marry?) and in no time he'll be ready to reload.

If he cries out in anguish and begins to search for a handgun you have a deeper kind of depression on your hands. Handling this correctly is a bit more difficult. Baby him, soothe his ego, and tell him everything will be okay. Try to make sure he doesn't fall into a deep funk, pulling out clumps of his hair or weeping openly in public restrooms. Men can be so sulky.

If it happens *more* frequently, it is permissable, (and advisable) to bring any of those standard sex guides to bed to work on his technique. You know the ones, *Joy of Sex, More Joy of Sex, Sex 'til Your Parts Are Raw and Blistered,* etc. Having him try to think of baseball won't work, besides, do you really want him thinking of Joaquin Andujar while you're making love?

If, after all this, he continues to let you down and refuses to try to alter his behavior to satisfy you, help him look for the gun.

Q: I believe my wife and I have a satisfying sexual relationship, but I can never tell if she climaxes or not. Is there a polite way to ask, "Was it good for you?"

A: If you have to ask, it wasn't.

Q: Well, then, suppose I can tell it was good but I'd like a little more vocal support? How do I ask for that?

A: Frankly, it's just not polite to ask. You might encourage her with some histrionics of your own, but some ladies are used to more genteel behavior. They may be put off if, at a crucial moment, you yell "Go, you wild heifer! Ride me like a bucking bronco!"

Q: I love having sex with my boyfriend, but he has a habit of talking and yelling and screaming during the more exciting portions of the act. I'm glad he's having a good time but it kind of throws my concentration off. Is it polite to make that much noise? Is there a polite way for me to ask him to cool it?

A: It is perfectly correct to vocalize during love making as long as no one but the participants can hear. Try to imagine how funny it would be to hear, "Oh, Glen, do me again with your big missile of love" coming through the heating vent from the apartment next door. Especially if your next door neighbor's husband's name is Roger.

There is probably no way to ask him to be quiet without hurting his feelings. You could say, "Hey, could we do this just once without you making sounds like a gored rhinocerous?" But that would be very rude. "Put a sock in it, Paul Revere," would be effective but nasty.

Q: Is it polite to have sex in ways besides the missionary position?" My wife seems shocked at the suggestion.

A: Not only is it polite it's damned important if you expect to stay interested in having sex at all after two weeks or so.

The "missionary position" is so named for religious zealots who tried to convert native Africans to Christianity in the early 1800's.

This was a very silly and dangerous thing to do but obviously these people were socially maladjusted. Why else would they be missionaries.?

They tried to convince the tribespeople that God smiled on only one sexual position, the man-on-top-hurry-up-and-get-it-over-with position. They taught the natives that sex was for procreation only and not for fun. The natives, who were used to running about naked and leaping on each other any time and any way they damn well pleased realized quickly that the missionaries were complete "foondarbs" (foondarb was the tribespeoples word for "pain-in-the-ass religious wieners who never get laid.") When the missionaries persisted they were tied to a spit, spread-eagled and face-down, and lightly grilled over an open flame. Thus the "missionary position," and the "barbeque," were born.

This was a harsh fate for the missionaries but let's face it. What would you do if some goof came into your bedroom and started telling you and your spouse what you could and could not do? Maybe you wouldn't make them into a casserole but you'd be very unhappy.

Religious types seem to be very fond, these days, of telling everyone what God smiles on and what he doesn't, especially when it comes to sex.

Consider that God has fixed it so that the only way to propagate the species is to get naked with someone of the opposite gender and rub these strange and difficult to locate parts together. He's also fixed it so people actually love to do it. So much so, that they spend all their time doing it, plotting how to do more of it, or remembering back to when they used to do it all the time. Next time you're locked in some acrobatic carnal embrace with your loved one, try to picture how you look to an observer. And you think God doesn't have a sense of humor?

Anyway, back to your query. *All* positions are polite. Funny, but polite. Have fun, and make sure you do some stretching exercises first. We don't want any sprains or pulled muscles out there.

Q: My husband likes to be on top all the time. But it's better for me when I'm on top. Can I demand equal time?

A: There is only one real sexual etiquette problem. That is, having sex with the wrong person. Unfortunately, you can't tell this bozo to take a hike without calling a lawyer and no one needs that kind of headache.

It is certainly correct for you to demand to be treated to a wonderful sexual experience every time. That's *every* time, men.

There is no rule of etiquette that prevents you from using several different positions during the same act. The thing to do is climb on top of him first. When he complains tell him it's your turn first and he can be next. If he objects, reach behind you and gently cradle his testicles in your hand. This should be very pleasurable for him and he should calm right down. If he continues to object, or tries to change positions, simply make your hand into a fist. I guarantee his attitude will change immediately.

Q: **What about "doggie style"? It seems so crude and animal-like. My wife seems to like it a lot but it's kind of hard for me to get into it. Is it really proper?**

A: As I said, all positions are acceptable. Pick up a copy of the Kama Sutra for a full listing.

Remember to have fun with them. Put blinders on her and get yourself a riding crop. Pretend you're Willie Shoemaker in the home stretch of the Kentucky Derby. (God, I love to imagine you people actually doing this stuff.)

Q: **My partner and I enjoy oral sex a great deal, both giving and receiving. Occasionally though, while receiving, I'll feel the rumblings of gastronomical distress. Is there a polite way to excuse myself from the proceedings until it "passes?"**

A: No, there isn't. You can, however, refrain from horking down two chili-cheeseburgers with everything in the hours preceeding the activity.

You might also want to visit your local bookstore and pick up a copy of "How to Stop Farting in 10 Days or Your Money Back" by my good friend and colleague, Dr. Herbert K. Poltweed. Sounds like you, and your poor partner, need it.

Q: **After some initial disenchantment with the practice, my girlfriend has become an avid practitioner of oral sex. As a matter of fact, she now prefers it to the exclusion of almost all other sexual activity. She tries to unzip my pants in theaters, on the highway, in restaurants...just about anywhere. What should I do about this?**

A: End this relationship immediately. Your girlfriend needs the kind of close personal guidance that only a trained professional can provide. Forward her name, address and phone number to me, care of the publisher.

Is Polite Orgasm Possible?
A Test

Which of the following words or phrases are correct to cry out during orgasm?

Place a P (Polite) or an I (Impolite) next to each phrase. Give yourself one point for each correct answer. (Answers below.)

_____ 1. Whip me, beat me, make me write bad checks!

_____ 2. Oh my goodness gracious, isn't this pleasant.

_____ 3. This is almost as much fun as a trip to Bloomies!

_____ 4. Don't worry, I'll pay for the dry cleaning.

_____ 5. Well, I'm finished. How 'bout you?

_____ 6. Wow, you're almost as good as my ex-husband.

_____ 7. Ouch, are those your toenails?

_____ 8. See, I told you size doesn't matter!

_____ 9. You know you're only the 23rd man who has been able to make me climax.

_____10. I love you.

All replies are considered impolite except 2. Number 10 may be very polite in some situations but can get you in lots of trouble.

POLITE AFTERPLAY
The Wet Spot and Other Dilemmas

*When choosing between two evils, I always like to try the one
I've never tried before.*

—Mae West

AFTERPLAY
The Wet Spot and Other Dilemmas

As we have discussed, men and women differ extravagantly in their approach to foreplay, orgasm and life in general. This, naturally, leads to tremendous etiquette dilemmas. So does the fact that women seem to require so much more winding down after climax.

After sex, women want you to whisper sweet things to them, stroke their silky hair and generally behave like a newborn puppy for about eight hours. They want to be tickled, pampered and held meaningfully. They want discreet ladies in waiting to bring in champagne breakfasts. They want their man to stroll unselfconsciously naked to the window, muscles rippling in the moonlight, sigh deeply and say, "God, that was wonderful...and you, you're wonderful." They want weekends in Aruba. They want thin thighs, unlimited bank accounts and calorie free chocolate. They want love. They want passion. They want romance. They want there to be no wet spot.

Men, on the other hand, want to sleep.

Q: Once I get started I could just go on forever. My husband, though, is strictly a one shot man. Is it good manners for me to demand more from him?

A: Unlike your friendly neighborhood vibrator, you can't just flip a man's switch to turn him on. Flip his switch 40 or 50 times in rapid succession and you might be able to, though.

Sex is a learned behavior. If he's used to dropping off to sleep after the act, it's going to take some time to get him to break the pattern. You could have a pre-sex talk with him. You could keep him from drinking too much beforehand. You could threaten to seduce the bag boy at the Piggly Wiggly.

Q: How long does he need to recuperate before I can ask for a replay?

A: There is a very simple formula for calculating this. It is directly related to age. At age 20 allow him 20 minutes for recuperation. At age 30 he'll need 30 minutes. At 40 he'll need 40 and at 50 he'll need 50.

At this point the formula begins to break down. If you're married to a man in his sixties, don't expect him to service you every hour on the hour. Unless, of course, you're a blushing young bride and you wish to be a blushing young widow.

It is considered very bad form to whip out a stopwatch immediately following the tender act of lovemaking and begin staring threateningly at his slumbering unit.

Q: Well, suppose while he recuperates I, uh, entertain myself with my vibrator? Wouldn't that be okay?

A: It's okay with me but it might be kind of discouraging for him. After he collapses, spent, sweat-soaked and nearing heart-failure following a couple of hours of manic love-making, you want to disturb his nap by inducing with your little handtool cries of ecstasy he could never hope to draw from you himself? You cruel, heartless woman.

Q: Well. . .so I'm a sexual dynamo, what am I supposed to do when he's finished and I'm not?

A: Use some tact, Vampira. Wait until he's asleep and sneak into the bathroom with it. Or go out to the car. Some of these newer models plug right into the cigarette lighter.

Q: All these questions are from women. When I get done with *my* woman *she's* the one who falls asleep. I'm always ready for more action. What do *I* do?

A: Quit yanking my chain, studmobile. Nobody believes that garbage for a minute.

CAN LIVING TOGETHER EVER BE POLITE?
Manners, Marriage and the Multiple Orgasm

Marriage is a great institution, but I'm not ready for an institution yet.

—Mae West

CAN LIVING TOGETHER EVER BE POLITE?

Manners, Marriage and the Multiple Orgasm

The answer to this profound query is, as you may have suspected, no, so don't do it. Now I know you're all destined to ignore my advice on this but I will elaborate anyway. Men and women were not meant to live together without benefit of clergy. And certainly not without benefit of separate bedrooms. I suspect that they were not meant to live together at all but I am a curmudgeonly type and am frequently given to notions like that.

Marriage is a sacred vow. A promise that binds two people in love together and makes it really difficult for them to split up without lawyers. Even if you find that you hate each other three days into the honeymoon, it'll be too embarrassing to give all those gifts back. And besides, it would give way too much pleasure to all your maiden aunts who clucked, "It'll never last."

So you'll get through the honeymoon and your hate will mellow into mild annoyance and you'll find that divorce is just too much trouble. After all, there are lawyers and alimony and who-gets-to-keep-the-stereo and, well, who needs it? Besides you get to have sex anytime you want.

Most people go on like this for years until something really horrible happens that finally renders the union   irreconcilable. Like she finds his freshly clipped toe nails under the coffee table. Or he finds her "X-pando" girdle brief hanging on the shower curtain rod for the

400th time. You will each hire a lawyer who specializes in taking advantage of people in their times of crisis and split everything down the middle. (That's why it's wise to have an even number of children.) You'll sell the house to one of those sick people who attend seminars that tell them how to make a fortune in real estate by buying up houses from people dealing with a death or divorce. You'll end up in apartments less than three blocks from each other. You will become better friends divorced than you were when you were married.

By this time, all your friends will be either separated, divorced or cheating, so you can finally fulfill all the carnal fantasies you developed in years of drunken back yard barbeques with the Lawrences, Smiths and McCabes. You'll finally find out if Kitty McCabe really got those implants, or if Norm was just talking.

This cycle will repeat itself about every ten years until the men join country clubs and die, leaving their widows to frost their hair blue, vacation in Palm Springs, and chat about their late husbands.

The lawyers retain a third and the real estate people get a percentage. This is God's plan so don't screw around with it.

Naturally there are those of you who will ignore my sage advice and choose to live in sin anyway. Shame on you.

Q: I moved in with my boyfriend six months ago and everything has been pretty good except that he does some things that just gross me out! Like he sits in the bathroom with the door open! It's so rude! How do I ask him politely to clean up his act?!

A: This sort of behavior is not considered polite even in today's permissive environment. However, just because he is behaving rudely doesn't give you the right to be impolite in turn. Your problem is, you moved in with this man before you checked out his personal habits. Men are inordinately proud of their bodies. That includes any liquids, gases or solids that their bodies may produce. And, they rarely have any compunction about producing these liquids, gases and solids in mixed company. He may actually ask you to come into the bathroom and have a look. He'll be hurt if you decline. It may have something to do with Mommy and toilet training. I'm sure Freud covered it somewhere in detail. In any case, men are almost universally talented when it comes to belching, farting and making other disgusting noises and smells. Keep plenty of Ozium on hand and never respond when he says, "Hey, honey, super bean dip. Here, pull my finger."

Q: **When we first moved in together the sex was frequent and terrific. Now, it's all I can do to get him to shut off David Letterman for a few minutes. Is it polite to ask him what happened?**

A: Well, you can certainly ask, but I doubt if you'll get a decent answer. The fact is, boredom sets in more easily than many of us are prepared to admit. Besides, Letterman is pretty good, especially that Man-Under-the-Seats bit.

However, if you bathed, powdered and primped, dolled yourself up in black net hose, garter-belt, peek-a-boo bra and high heels, strutted into the bedroom in a cloud of musk and said, "Hi, big guy, my name is Mona the Man-Eater and I can suck a tennis ball through a chain-link fence," I bet you'd get some action.

On the other hand, that Paul Schaefer really cracks me up.

Q: **What can I say to politely discourage my mate when he's obviously in an amorous mood and I'm not?**

A: It's not so much what you say but how you say it. Sex, as we all know should be a cosmic, earth-shattering experience for all parties involved. Well, it should at least be a pleasant way to spend six or seven minutes for all parties involved. If one party has horrific gas pains or a debilitating rash or is just not in the mood, that party can certainly decline to participate. A simple, "Gosh, sugar drawers, I just don't feel up to it right now," should be sufficient to quell the advances of a reasonably sensitive male. Well, I guess I shouldn't forget that we're talking about men here. Men normally want to have sex about once an hour even if they have bad gas or a rash. The only time they don't want it is when they're eating, sleeping, watching "The Dukes of Hazzard," or when you want it.

Let's say your man is stalking about the house cradling a throbbing erection in his hand and he says to you, "Just hold still and close your eyes. It'll only take a minute." You are allowed to use a garden hose on him.

Q: My husband is always grabbing at me in public places. I don't mind the attention but sometimes he just goes too far. How do I know what's rude and what isn't?

A: Men have a tremendous fondness for toys and to them your various parts are their own little playground. They will grope you, nibble you, pinch you and tickle you constantly, at opportune and inopportune times. If you are blessed with rather large breasts (use the pencil test if you're not sure) your man will happily and distractedly slop them back and forth in wonderment for hours. Much like a baby playing with a rattle.

Men will also amuse themselves with your erectile tissue in public places. This is tremendously rude, especially if you're at a dinner party for your biggest client. If he pinches your nipple in this situation the correct thing to do is wink at him and ask him to join you in the kitchen. As he walks in with a wide grin on his face, anticipating a "quickie," smile sweetly and dump the relish tray down his pants. This is perfectly proper behavior.

Be forewarned, though, your man is very proud of your erect nipples and will often attempt to get you to stand under air conditioning vents, near the frozen food aisle and in front of the meat cooler at the grocery store. This is slightly rude but essentially harmless and the butcher may be impressed enough to save you the leaner cuts.

GROOMING
Our Bodies, Our Smells

Many a man has fallen in love with a girl in a light so dim he would not have chosen a suit by it.

                                                    —*Maurice Chevalier*

GROOMING
Our Bodies, Our Smells

Men, as has been previously pointed out, rarely give any thought to their appearance. Or smell, for that matter. (When I say men, I mean heterosexual men. Gay men are very neat *except* when it comes to their sexual practices.)

Most men will blithely don green checked "Sans-a-Belt" slacks, a brown striped shirt, pink tie with little blue anchors, and a robins-egg blue polyester jacket. They will be surprisedwhen you shriek in horror at the breakfast table. Men secretly believe it's macho to be a tasteless slob. Check his socks. They will be two different shades of brown and have holes in both heel and toe. These kinds of men may also suffer from a tremendous case of dandruff, shocking overuse of Brylcreme and almost uncorrectable nearsightedness. He may or may not brush his teeth monthly.

Okay, now despite these enormous obstacles, you have fallen in love with him. After all, you reason, he needs you. So you get him contact lenses, a blow-dryer, a wardrobe featuring colors actually found in nature, and some socially acceptable personal habits.

Are you really surprised to find this man wearing grey, frayed, de-elasticized, hole-y, pee-stained, 8-year-old Sears brand briefs? No, of course you're not.

Q: **That's exactly the kind of underwear my husband insists on wearing. What can I do?**

A: Even if you march him in front of the mirror and point out to him how ridiculous a grown man looks in this sort of underclothing, he will probably continue to cling to them. And vice versa. After all, his mom has been buying his little jockeys since he graduated from toilet training and he's not about to give them up. It's quite conceivable that your man has never actually bought underwear as an adult. He may be too embarrassed to do it. He will certainly be too embarrassed to stroll casually up to the counter at the K-Mart and hand the 17-year-old, gum-cracking cashier a 3-pack of low-rise mesh bikinis in assorted colors.

Besides, let's face it, a paunchy, shallow-chested man with in-grown hairs on his thighs looks even more ridiculous in a pair of peach colored bikini briefs than he does in his all-American shorts from Sears. And a man with panty lines that show is too hilarious for words.

Beware! If you do succeed in changing his mind about underwear, you may arrive home from work one day to find him sprawled out on the couch with a beer, in socks, baseball cap and knee-length *boxer shorts!* They may have very silly designs on them, perhaps little poodles jumping through a hoop or polka dots or, that all time favorite, big red hearts. He will probably be scratching himself.

For some reason, a man who would normally reserve the sight of himself clad in this way for you (you lucky girl) will suddenly become a wild exhibitionist when he begins wearing boxers. He will parade around shamelessly in front of your friends, neighbors, the baby sitter, your mother and your pot-luck group. Maybe his father did this and it's some sort of strange male bonding ritual. No one knows.

Anyway, boxers are usually only correct for men over fifty. They are always worn together with those strange sleeveless undershirts. Boxers can also be worn by young men from California who seem to think it's okay to wear underwear that sticks out the top and bottom of their shorts. People from California also think that alfalfa sprouts have some taste and that Tatum O'Neal has talent, so we may dismiss them from further discussion.

In short, when buying your man's underwear steer clear of the boxer shorts display. That's the kind of nightmare you don't need.

Another option is to suggest that your man "go Indian." That is, have nothing between him and his Calvin's. While some may consider this sexy it can be uncomfortable. Especially if he favors wool slacks. Or when it's 20° below. Or when he has an accident and has to go to the hospital.

Apparently that leaves us with but one sad conclusion. There is no acceptable underwear for men. Normal men, anyway. The blow dried, tanned models with the rippling stomach muscles featured in those upscale clothing catalogs look terrific in underwear of any kind. Even that ridiculous mesh stuff. The average man, of course, looks as little like one of these men than the average woman looks like Linda Evans. Of course, when off-camera you can be sure that even *these* men wear the same grey, frayed, de-elasticized, hole-y, pee-stained, 8-year-old, Sears brand briefs that their Moms bought for them. Unless they're homosexual. Which brings us back to where we were before.

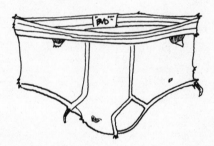

Q: My husband wants me to wear fancy lingerie and garter belts and stuff. I don't want to. It's uncomfortable and it makes me feel silly besides. I don't think it's polite for him to pressure me to, do you?

A: While women enjoy a myriad of choices when it comes to their underclothing they quite frequently end up behaving the same way most men do. You sneer at your husbands old shorts yet, at the same time, how many times do you end up pulling on those old cotton panties with Mickey Mouse on the front? Or the ones you got from your boyfriend in college that say "Go You Sun Devils" across the butt?

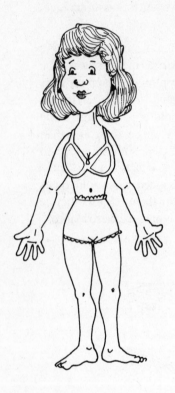

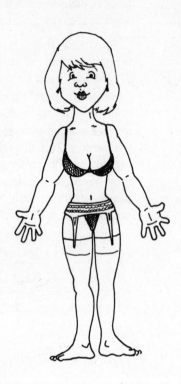

Can you tell the married lady from the single lady simply by viewing their undergarments?

Fill in the blank.

Although guilty of wearing raggedy drawers on occasion, women generally *are* more conscientious than men about their undergarments. In fact, entire industries have been built around women and their drawers. Look through any Frederick's of Hollywood or Victoria's Secret catalog and you'll find page after page filled with willowy, curvaceous women clothed only in a seductive smile and (pick one): lace camisole, strapless satin bodice, black boudoir top, leopard striped bodysuit, garter belt, antique lace bustier, fish net stockings, white lace teddy, crotchless black panties, red G-string, front hook, sheer, push-up bra, or string bikini . . . in any combination. These women use two tubes of Nair a week.

In fact, it is a rare woman, outside these catalogs and a few Las Vegas hotel lounges, that *ever* wears this stuff. Oh, they may go so far as to purchase a rather high cut pair of panties once in a while, but, for the most part, these catalogs and chain stores cater to the fantasies and tastes of the average male. Most women feel faintly ridiculous in an outfit that contains more buttons, hooks and silk than the average parachute pack.

The fact is, men, while you're dating, the woman of your dreams will wear all the enticing underwear you want. It makes her feel sexy, happy and in love. Once you make a permanent commitment, however, she will immediately pack all her sexy lingerie in a cardboard box, write ARBOR DAY DECORATIONS on it with a Marks-a-lot, and stuff it in the crawl space. From that day forward she will buy and wear only "married lady underwear." Married lady underwear are what the Sears catalog calls "briefs" or "hipsters." They come in pink, white and pale yellow. They are all cotton and cover the woman from the navel on down. Your grandmother used to call underwear like these "bloomers." They are comfortable. They breathe. They are boring.

She calls them "underpants." by the way. No woman in recorded history ever calls her underwear "panties."

Basically, everyone in the free-world buys their underwear at Sears. That's what makes Sears stock such a good investment. What I'm getting at is that, while dressing up as a hormone drenched Carmen Miranda is a bit much, it couldn't hurt to do the G-string and garter belt thing for your husband once in a while. Don't be so modest! He'll be too busy being your love slave to notice the varicose veins on your calves or the orange-rind-like texture of your outer thighs.

Q: My wife wants me to wear these here little bikini deals she bought. Hell, I ain't wearin' these fag drawers! They came in a plastic tube fer Chrissakes!

A: Now, now, if you expect your wife to look attractive for you, you're going to have to reciprocate. (That means, "Y'all gotta do the same fer the little lady.") The rule of etiquette that applies: "Do whatever makes your partner happy as long as it's only mildly painful and humiliating." It's only fair that you try to please her. If, however, she takes Polaroids of you in a G-string and cherry-red pumps and shows them to your bowling team you may break her legs.

Q: My husband wants me to shave my pubic hair. I'm very offended by this request and I think it's rude of him to ask me.

A: There are no rules of etiquette forbidding crotch shaving. You may find it distasteful and may refuse to succumb to your husband's request, of course. Some men *and* some women like this sort of thing and it's really pretty harmless. It may be difficult for him to explain to the boys at the office later, though, how *he* got a whisker burn from *you*.

Q: What if he wants me to trim it into the shape of something?

A: As I said previously, to your man your body is nothing so much as his little playground. Should he, in a drunken, passionate moment, approach your crotch with a scissors, babbling about the heart shaped pubic thatch sported by Joy Ryde in "Wild Pussycats from the Planet Hormone," it is perfectly proper to lock him in the closet until his tonsorial ardor cools.

Some more adventurous ladies, though, enjoy doing this. They find it exciting to know that under their prim, pin-striped business suit and sensible underwear lurks a small fuzzy heart, arrow or (my favorite) bulls-eye. If you *are* into this though, be careful! It

is very difficult to explain to the overnight resident at the emergency room why you need five stitches in your lower abdomen. Keep that tetanus booster up-to-date just in case.

Q: My husband is quite hairy, if you know what I mean. I try to get him to do something about it but he says that "real men don't shave." I don't know, I think it's gross.

A: Men are far from exempt from crotch trimming, although from the looks of some of the European style bathing suits I have been unfortunate to have seen lately, many believe that they are. For goodness sake, people! Let's clean it up! There are not, unfortunately, simple guidelines for men, especially when so many seemed to be covered with body hair of various thickness from throat to ankle. The correct thing to do is use common sense, be neat, and remember, the more you trim the bigger you'll look. (That ought to send them for the weed-eater.)

Q: My girlfriend is wildly passionate once the lights are out, but otherwise she's so shy it drives me nuts! Would it be rude for me to demand at least occasional lighted love making?

A: There is something very important about women's bodies that all men need to know. (No, it's not where to find the G Spot.) That is, that all women, regardless of how beautiful, believe that their bodies are ugly. They secretly believe that if they stand in front of you, naked, in daylight, you will turn, screaming, and catch a train to Boise. They feel this way because Hugh Hefner, Bob Guccione and legions of advertising executives have spent the last thirty or forty years parading unblemished, unscarred, anorexic, airbrushed images of fantasy females before the eyes of males everywhere.

Even if you were to find yourself, through some strange twist of fate, before a naked Playmate of the Year, in the throes of heated passion and you were to declare that you wished to be her love slave for the rest of the century because of her blinding beauty, she would say, "Oh, no. I'm much too (use any of the following): Fat, skinny, short, tall, flat-chested, top-heavy, knock-kneed, bow-legged, dark, light, freckled, flabby, hippy, etc., etc., etc.

No woman can accept a compliment about her naked self. Years of conditioning assure this. If you tell her she's gorgeous she will assume it's because you are consumed with animal lust and would jump a crocodile if you could get it to hold still.

There *is* a Catch-22 in all this. You see, women get livid if you don't compliment them on their appearance frequently. The solution? Make a fuss over her *only* when she's fully dressed.

The same woman who believes that she is tremendously flawed when naked will be mortally offended if you don't notice how cleverly she has concealed those flaws with make-up, hair-do and brilliant taste in clothes. The polite, and wise, move is to compliment her excessively at these times. Magazines like Cosmo, Glamour and Madamoiselle make a fortune advertising these kinds of products while at the same time running articles like, "Why Your Nose Is Wrong for Your Face" and "Get That Promotion and Change Your Whole Miserable Existence by Flattening Your Tummy in Just 30 Days." This confirms a theory of mine that magazines are responsible for all the unrest in America today. Cancel your subscriptions, bring a book to the doctor's office and stay out of grocery check out lines. You'll feel better. Trust me.

Q: Well, you're right. My wife does act like that a lot. What do I do about it?

A: Of course I'm right! I'm an expert! Boy, sometimes. Now, you could try saying the following: "I love you, sweetheart, and when *I* look at you I'm looking at the most beautiful woman on the face of this Earth."

Try not to snicker. It will ruin the effect.

Q: My husband seems to think it's all right to come to bed without bathing. Now, I don't demand that he be completely bacteria free but I think *some* consideration is in order, don't you?

A: Men, unlike you modest ladies, seem to feel that they are tremendously attractive no matter what condition they're in. Even after he's finished a softball tournament in 90 degree heat, devoured

a large pepperoni, onion, mushroom, green pepper and anchovy pizza *and* three pitchers of beer. This man will lurch into your bedroom clad in a damp jockstrap and dirt, belch loudly and declare, "It's me, the Prince of Passion and I'm here to take you to Ecstasy Land." This, you may have gathered, is not at all polite, but is worth a few laughs.

ACCESSORIES
Good Vibrations

Oh, wouldn't you be in good shape, if your life was on videotape?

—Steve Goodman

ACCESSORIES
Good Vibrations

Many of you reading this, I know, consider yourselves more "adventurous" than most. Perhaps you read the table of contents and skipped ahead to read this chapter first. Shame on you.

You couples view yourselves as "open minded" and "fun." You use hot oils, flavored, edible undergarments, vibrators and assorted other "marital aids" to distract you from the fact that making love the same partner for 20 straight years is about as exciting as the farm report.

So you ingest bizarre drugs, watch x-rated video tapes, look at dirty pictures and smear various foodstuffs on each other in a pitiful attempt to pump some cheap thrills into your desperately dull sex lives.

Do I paint a grim picture?

Does Seka wear knee pads?

The variety of sex aid products now on the market truly boggles the mind. Many can be obtained through colorful catalogs which feature such indispensible items as strap on dildos, anal stimulators, condoms of all shapes, sizes, textures and colors, and lubricants for every imaginable orifice. It is hard to know how to deal gracefully with these things.

For you loners and free spirits, who love the thrill of exciting sex but hate those awkward complications that can occur when you include another human being, there are numerous kinds of autoerotic devices. Some include special attachments for clitoral stimulating, anal vibrating, drapery cleaning and sparkplug changing. What great stocking stuffers these handy little items make! And don't forget to include extra batteries. You don't want to be frantically disemboweling

Junior's new Masters of the Universe™ Slime Pit on Christmas Eve night in a desperate search for two working Duracels.

Sex oils and lubricants can be lots of fun, too. Who wants to taste skin when you can taste "banana nut fudge ripple" hot love oil?

Is the use of these kinds of adult toys ill-mannered? Not really. Not as long as everyone seems to be having a good time. Still, it's always wise to use caution with these products. It is *not* polite to clamp the "super sta-hard erecto-ring" on your man's member when he's not looking. And even the most adventurous woman might be a bit taken aback if you charge at her out of the closet armed with the electric "Four-headed Gorgon of love."

Be cautious also in your use of flavored oils and douches. We smell and taste the way we do because it's exciting and attractive to the opposite sex. Tamper too much with natural chemistry by using your man's favorite strawberry douche and you may find him one day attempting oral sex with the slushee machine at your local convenience store.

Q: Is it polite for me to use a vibrator? How do I introduce the subject to my husband?

A: Ah, modern technology. Betcha Grandma never had this problem. There is no polite way to tell your husband that his equipment, technique and love-making ability are inadequate. No really correct way to say that you'd rather have a 12" hunk of humming plastic inside you than him.

If you must use one of these admittedly effective little monsters, at least wait until he's out at bowling night.

Let's compare now. A healthy, mature man can deliver approximately 25 to 45 SPM's (strokes per minute) for about five minutes. If he goes longer than that he's either been drinking, he's bored, or he was masturbating earlier in the day.

An imaginative man can provide anywhere from one to a dozen nice orgasms for his lover over the course of the evening.

On the other hand (excuse the pun) "Mr. Space Shot" and a fresh supply of Evereadys can deliver 2000 SPM's for about five months and will make it possible for you to climax about 38 times an hour or until you pass out.

Do you really want someone you care about to have to compete with that?

Q: **My husband wants me to watch X-rated movies with him. He says they'll turn me on. I've never seen one before but they sure sound gross. Are videos considered acceptable sex toys?**

A: Until recently, conventional thinking had it that most women did not find X-rated films or photos sexually stimulating. Men liked to believe that women were aroused by things like personality or the ability to build model airplanes or complete acrostic puzzles, not bulging biceps and sleek, firm pectorals. This was convenient for men because it allowed them to rationalize looking like Ralph Kramden.

Most X-rated films are conceived by men, produced by men, written by men and directed by men. They usually star several heavily made-up women with the combined IQ and acting abilities of Morris the Cat. They usually have bleached blonde hair and breasts the size of bean bag chairs. They sport titles like "Hose Bag Heaven" and "If My Thighs Had Eyes." Is it any surprise that few women find these films arousing?

Porn makers realize that the bulk of the viewers of these movies are bad smelling, unshaven, sexually desperate men who order inflatable dolls through the mail. The entire porn industry is supported by these men who watch the videos in their seedy little rooms and masturbate frantically into wet washcloths. It is estimated that they are also responsible for 63% of VCR sales in this country over the last six years.

Q: **My husband wants to make a videotape of us making love. Is that considered proper?**

A: Taking photos of yourselves or making a tape can be great fun and today's sophisticated equipment makes it possible to get really high quality. This is especially important for after your divorce when he wants to show it to his softball team.

Making a tape of yourselves is also great for contraceptive purposes. Just the sight of you two pale, flabby people squirming around on top of each other and grunting like wild pigs in a feeding frenzy should be enough to make you swear off sex forever.

Q: Is there really any such thing as an aphrodisiac? I am madly in love with a woman who is rather cool to me and I'd love to find something to drop in her coffee.

A: First of all, it is tremendously rude to drop something in someone's coffee unless they've asked you to. Besides that, there is no such thing as "Spanish Fly" or any other little magic pill. Stories about "love potions" and such abound but the fact is there is only one true, 100% never fail aphrodisiac for women:

Directions for use: Place $100 bill in her outstretched palm. Repeat with additional bills until she rips off her clothing and cries out, "God, I want to smother you with my sweet hot monkey love!!" Size of the dosage will depend a great deal on *your* height, weight, and the kind of car you drive.

Q: **I've been trying to interest my wife in a "menage a tróis." She doesn't think she'd like it very much. Aren't groups of three or more okay?**

A: Men love the idea of being so sexually appealing that they can satisfy more than one woman. It's a very common fantasy. Men especially love the idea of "women together." Bob Guccione built a financial empire by publishing photos of "women together." We'd probably sell a lot more of *these* books if we had included lots of photos of "women together." These are not lesbians, mind you. To men, lesbians are squat, ill-tempered females who wear flannel shirts and army pants and are too ugly to get a man. "Women together" is a whole different concept. "Women together" means two beautiful, lithe, mainly heterosexual women who are so sexually charged that they become slaves to their own desires *and* to the man having the fantasy.

Be careful about living out this fantasy men! Face it, if you were ever actually able to round up two women to have sex with, you'd be so excited you'd probably last about 18 seconds. Then your two little playmates would have to entertain each other while you recuperated. Do you really think you can satisfy a woman better than another woman can? Forget it. Women are smooth, gentle, good-smelling creatures who always wear clean underwear. You, on the other hand, are a lumpy, hairy, evil smelling creature who snores. You've got enough problems competing with the "Mr. Vibromatic" you bought her and the "Jack, the Three Legged Man" videotape you brought home. You don't need a multi-orgasmic, bisexual nymph with a six inch tongue around to make you feel even less secure.

Luckily for you, many women are appalled at the thought of having sex with another woman. If you suggest a threesome she may assume that you mean adding another guy. Maybe she's had her eye on the refrigerator repairman who is also an amateur body builder. Do you really want to have sex with your lover while a mini Arnold Schwarzenegger stands there naked displaying an erection the size of a fire hose? Don't torture yourself.

SEX, DRUGS AND ROCK AND ROLL
The Straight Dope

A woman drove me to drink...and I never even had the courtesy to thank her.

—W.C. Fields

SEX, DRUGS AND ROCK 'N ROLL
The Straight Dope

Mind altering substances have been a tool of the art of seduction since cavemen figured out that it was easier to attract those cave gals with a little fermented logan berry juice than it was to bash them with blunt objects. Made for more exciting sex, too.

A little booze before sex seems traditional at this point. It's essentially harmless and it seems to help get everyone in the mood. But don't overdo it! There's little that's less attractive to your date than watching you barf the nice dinner he bought you. Remember, though, these things sometimes happen. Men, if you really care about etiquette you'll hold her hair back while she pukes. She'll love you for it.

Nowadays, of course, there are dozens of drugs available to anyone silly enough to risk imprisonment and public humiliation by taking them. There *are* those couples who insist that a little dope makes lovemaking more of a pleasure or that a little speed or cocaine make it more exciting. It's difficult for me to fathom how sex between two glazed, comatose, and/or babbling people could be very exciting.

Q: My husband always has a few drinks, usually beer, before we have sex. He says it makes him "last longer." It may be true, but is it polite?

A: You're husband is probably right. Alcohol, like many drugs, does deaden the nerves a bit. It will make him less "sensitive" and that should be extra nice for you. A friend of mine, who is normally far too crude for me to pay any attention to at all, has a name for this condition. He calls it "whiskey dick." Crude, as I said, but accurate.

Q: Is there anything really wrong with smoking a little grass grass before sex? I love it and I know it makes the sex better. My boyfriend, however, says it's insulting to him. Is it?

A: Well, let's see. What you're telling the man you love is this. "I can't bear to let you touch me with your slimy hands unless I've smoked myself into oblivion first." Yeah, I think that could be considered just a little insulting.

Dope deadens the nerve endings too, you see. I would think that sex with deadened nerve endings would be like...well...sex with deadened nerve endings. And if it takes too long to complete the act you'll probably lose interest and start dialing Gianni's for a large pepperoni, extra cheese. A man could become a bit miffed at this kind of treatment.

Q: What about cocaine? My girlfriend insists that "Things come better with coke."

A: Cocaine is an even more potent aphrodisiac than cold cash because it makes a statement. The statement it makes is "I have lots of money and I'm eager to spend it foolishly." That's the kind of statement so many women just love to hear.

There seems to be a great deal of interest in this subject so I've gone to great trouble and expense to prepare the following chart. Cut it out and keep it in your wallet.

SEX AND DRUGS

	DRUG	GENERAL EFFECT
MAN		Bravado
	Alcohol	
WOMAN		Accessible
MAN		Zoned Out
	Marijuana	
WOMAN		Accessible
MAN		Hallucinations
	LSD	
WOMAN		Accessible
MAN		Bright, Witty Runny nose
	Cocaine	
WOMAN		Accessible
MAN		Talkative
	Speed	
WOMAN		Accessible
MAN		Dopey
	Quaaludes	
WOMAN		Accessible

A HELPFUL CHART

PREFERRED SEX ACT	TIME	AFTERPLAY
Man on top	20 Minutes	ZZZZZ
Woman on top		Throw Up.
Woman on top	2 Hours	Pigout on brownies, pizza curls, and butter pecan ice cream.
Man on top		
Rolling around in pit of snakes and flaming space ships.	Doesn't matter; you'll never be able to touch anyway.	Sit and watch as you each change into giant lizards.
Snorting coke off each other's privates.	Until the coke's gone.	Go get some more coke.
All of them	38 Seconds	Find some Quaaludes
Shopping		
You'll have forgotten how	All weekend	Throw Up.

ZZZZZ |

ABOUT THE AUTHOR

Tom Carey is a writer and illustrator in Chicago whose previously published work includes *"The Nun Book," "The One Minute Gynecologist," "The I Love to Fart Cookbook"* and *"How to Stop Farting in 10 Days."*

His parents think he sells computer software.